5 STEPS TO A 5™

AP Psychology

2023

ELITE STUDENT EDITION

5 STEPS TO A 5

AP Psychology

2023

Laura Lincoln Maitland, MA, MSEd
Laura Sheckell, MA

Mc
Graw
Hill

New York Chicago San Francisco Athens London Madrid
Mexico City Milan New Delhi Singapore Sydney Toronto

CONTENTS

PREFACE

Welcome to the new edition of this test preparation book for AP Psychology that includes information from *DSM-5*. If you don't know what *DSM-5* is, you will soon. The book has been designed so that it is user-friendly and employs the concepts psychologists know about learning and remembering to help you succeed. Each chapter begins with an advance organizer to help you understand the material. Smaller sections enable you to fit what you are learning into the framework of what you already know. Features that previous users found most helpful, such as the definitions in the glossary at the end of the book, questions very similar to those actually on the AP exam, and Rapid Review at the end of each content chapter have been retained.

If psychology were mainly common sense, as many people think, you wouldn't need this book. You wouldn't need to study either. In fact, many concepts in psychology are counterintuitive, the opposite of what common sense leads us to think. Actually, psychology is a real science with a substantial knowledge base. If you are currently enrolled in an Advanced Placement Psychology course, you know how much more than listening to people's problems and analyzing them is included in the study of psychology, and you know how many hundreds of pages you need to navigate in a hard-covered course textbook. If you're not enrolled in an AP course, you may need additional support to help you select material that is likely to be tested on the May exam. In either situation, you'll benefit from this book, which was created to help you study for the Advanced Placement Exam in Psychology®.

This book provides you with the information on which you need to focus for taking the Advanced Placement Exam in Psychology® and gives you opportunities to practice answering AP-type questions. The multiple-choice questions count for two-thirds of your test score, and the essays count for one-third. While multiple-choice questions usually assess your understanding of one concept, essays test your understanding of numerous concepts and your ability to integrate information from more than one chapter. Practice in answering both multiple-choice and essay questions will help you do well on the AP exam. Read all the material and answer all the questions in all of the content chapters of this book, if you have enough time. Check your answers. Follow the study tips to help you learn and remember material you need to know. As the May exam approaches, take the two practice tests at the end of the book, and check your answers to see what you still need to learn. Since studying will help you succeed, it's time to get started!

ABOUT THE AUTHORS

Laura Lincoln Maitland received a BA in biological sciences from Douglass College, an MA in psychology from Stony Brook University, an MS in education from CUNY–Queens College, and a Professional Diploma from Long Island University.

Retired from the Bellmore-Merrick Central High School District, where she was lead science chairperson and taught Living Environment, AP Psychology, and Science Research for many years, she is currently an adjunct instructor at Hofstra University. She is also an education consultant at Cold Spring Harbor Laboratories, Long Island BOCES, and a variety of other venues. Laura has been a workshop presenter for the College Board, the New York State Biology-Chemistry Professional Development Network, Cold Spring Harbor Laboratory's Dolan DNA Learning Center, the Bellmore-Merrick Central High School District, the New York City Board of Education, and the New York State Education Department.

One of the founders and early chairs of Teachers of Psychology in Secondary Schools, she chaired the committee that created National Standards for High School Psychology Curricula. She also served on the AP Psychology Development Committee for the College Board/ETS. She received the first American Psychological Association Presidential Citation presented to a high school teacher and the American Psychological Association Division Two Excellence in Teaching Award.

Laura Sheckell studied psychology at the University of Michigan, where she received her BA in psychology. She continued her studies at the University of Michigan in secondary education with certification in social studies and psychology. Laura also received an MA in K–12 administrative education from Michigan State University.

Laura is currently teaching various psychology courses at Wylie E. Groves High School in Beverly Hills, Michigan, where she has spent 20 years as part of the Birmingham Public Schools system. The extensive psychology curriculum includes Psychology, Psychology and the Individual, AP Psychology, and Topics in Psychology. She has also served as the Social Studies Department chairperson for the past five years. Laura has been fortunate to work as an AP Psychology reader and table leader for College Board/ETS for 5 years.

INTRODUCTION: THE FIVE-STEP PROGRAM

The Basics

Learning, thinking, solving problems, and remembering are all psychological processes. To earn the highest score of 5 on the AP Psychology exam, you'll need to do them successfully! While the content sections of this book will help you understand concepts involved in learning and cognition, following the 5-step program will help you apply these concepts to maximize your success on the May exam.

Introducing the Five-Step Preparation Program

This book is organized as a 5-step program to prepare you to succeed on the exam. These steps are designed to provide you with vital skills and strategies and the practice that can lead you to that perfect 5. Here are the 5 steps.

Step 1: Set Up Your Study Program

In this step, you'll read a brief overview of the AP Psychology exam, including an outline of topics and the approximate percentage of the exam that will test knowledge of each topic. You will also follow a process to help determine which of the following preparation programs is right for you:

- Full school year: September through May.
- One semester: January through May.
- Six weeks: Basic training for the exam.

Step 2: Determine Your Test Readiness

In this step, you'll take a diagnostic multiple-choice exam in psychology. This pretest should give you an idea of how prepared you are to take the real exam before beginning to study for the actual AP Psychology Exam.

- Go through the diagnostic exam step by step and question by question to build your confidence level.
- Review the correct answers and explanations so that you see what you do and do not yet fully understand.

Step 3: Develop Strategies for Success

In this step, you'll learn strategies that will help you do your best on the exam. These strategies cover both the multiple-choice and free-response sections of the exam. Since serving on the College Board committee to design the first course of study and examinations for Advanced Placement Psychology, I have worked with many students and teachers who have helped me gain insight into how they think and study. Tasks that lull you into a false sense of security with shortcuts that may not work are NOT here.

- Learn to read multiple-choice questions.
- Learn how to answer multiple-choice questions.
- Learn how to plan and write the free-response questions.

Step 4: Review the Knowledge You Need to Score High

In this step, you'll learn or review the material you need to know for the test. This review section takes up the bulk of this book. It contains the following:

- A comprehensive review of introductory psychology.

Psychologists and educators do not agree on exactly what students should know after completing an introductory course in psychology, so no book can correctly forecast what concepts you need to know to get 100 percent of the questions on the AP exam right. But I can safely guarantee that this book includes the information that will enable you to earn a 5! The substantial knowledge you gain from studying it will significantly increase your chances of scoring well.

Step 5: Build Your Test-Taking Confidence

In this step, you'll complete your preparation by testing yourself on practice exams. I have provided you with two complete exams in psychology and scoring guides for them. Although these practice exams are *not* reproduced questions from actual AP Psychology exams, they mirror both the material tested by AP and the way in which it is tested.

Finally, at the back of this book you'll find additional resources to aid your preparation. These include the following:

- A brief bibliography.
- A list of websites related to the AP Psychology exam.
- A glossary of terms related to the AP Psychology exam.

Introduction to the Graphics Used in This Book

To emphasize particular skills and strategies, we use several icons throughout this book. An icon in the margin will alert you that you should pay particular attention to the accompanying text. We use these three icons:

 This icon points out a very important concept or fact that you should not pass over.

 This icon calls your attention to a strategy that you may want to try.

 This icon indicates a tip that you might find useful.

Boldfaced words indicate terms that are included in the glossary at the end of this book. Throughout the book you will also find marginal notes, boxes, and starred areas. Pay close attention to these areas because they can provide tips, hints, strategies, and further explanations to help you reach your full potential.

STEP 1

Set Up Your Study Plan

CHAPTER 1

What You Need to Know About the AP Psychology Exam

IN THIS CHAPTER

Summary: Learn what topics are tested, how the test is scored, and basic test-taking information.

Key Ideas

✪ AP Psychology is equivalent to a college-level introductory psychology course.

✪ Most, but not all, colleges will award credit for a score of 4 or 5.

✪ Multiple-choice questions account for two-thirds of your final score.

✪ There is NO penalty for guessing.

✪ Free-response questions account for one-third of your final score.

✪ Your composite score on the two test sections is converted to a score on the 1-to-5 scale.

Background Information

The College Board's Advanced Placement (AP) program enables high school students to study college-level subjects. Most colleges grant credit, placement, or both for qualifying AP exam grades. You may want to check with the colleges of your choice to find out their policies. Enrollment in AP Psychology has increased annually since its inception to become one of the most popular of 35 AP courses and exams offered.

Some Frequently Asked Questions About the AP Psychology Exam

Why Take the AP Psychology Exam?

AP Psychology is an exciting course to take not only because it gives you an opportunity to understand your own behavior and mental processes better but also because it enables you to learn more about other people and animals. Benefits of taking such a challenging course can include strengthening your transcript, proving to yourself that you can do it, and starting college with some credit. Admissions officers from Adelphi University to Yale University have told me that their number one criterion for admissions decisions is the strength of an applicant's high school program.

Additional benefits are sometimes offered. Some high schools weight or scale AP course grades. Because some colleges charge per credit, you can save money. Getting three or more credits for the price of the exam is a good value.

The College Board reports, "Studies have shown that AP students are more likely to maintain a high grade point average and graduate from college with honors than their college classmates of similar ability. . . ."

What Is the Format of the Exam?

Table 1.1 summarizes the format of the AP Psychology exam.

Table 1.1 AP Psychology

Section	Questions	Time Limit
I. Multiple-Choice Questions	100	1 hour 10 minutes (70 minutes)
II. Free-Response Questions	2	50 minutes

The exam is 2 hours long. During the first 70 minutes, you have 100 multiple-choice questions to answer. At the end of the 70 minutes, your booklet and answer sheet will be collected. However, no matter how early you finish this first part of the exam, you cannot begin the free-response questions (essays) early. The multiple-choice section counts for two-thirds of your score. If you have time remaining after you complete the questions, you can go back to those you were uncertain about or want to reread. You are limited to 50 minutes to answer two required essay questions.

Who Writes the AP Psychology Exam?

Development of each AP exam is a multiyear effort that involves many education and testing professionals and students. At the heart of the effort is the AP Psychology Development Committee, a group of highly regarded college and AP high school teachers from diverse backgrounds who are typically asked to serve for 3 years. The committee and experienced test-item writers create a large pool of multiple-choice questions. With the help of psychometricians (measurement psychologists) at Educational Testing Service (ETS), these questions are then pretested with college students who are enrolled in introductory psychology at selected colleges and universities. Questions are evaluated for accuracy, appropriateness, clarity, and assurance that there is only one possible answer. Data from pretests allow each question to be categorized by degree of difficulty.

In general, the easiest questions to answer are at the beginning of Section I, and the most difficult questions are at the end. After additional development and refinement, Section I of the exam is ready to be administered.

Numerous free-response questions (essay questions) are written for possible inclusion on the exams. After these questions are edited, discussed by committee members, and pretested with college psychology classes, the committee chooses essay questions for inclusion on a specific AP Psychology exam. They ensure that the free-response questions cut across content areas, are well presented and unambiguous, as well as considerably different from each other. Only free-response questions that will allow for clear and equitable grading by the AP readers (scorers) are selected.

After exams have been scored, the AP Psychology Development Committee and ETS evaluate the test results. The College Board can use the results to further course development in high schools and to plan future exams.

What Is Going to Appear on the Exam?

The College Board periodically surveys colleges/universities throughout the United States and around the world to find out what is being taught in introductory psychology courses in order to ensure that what is being taught in the AP course is comparable. The exam presumes the equivalent of at least one term/semester of college-level work.

Based on the latest information, the AP Psychology Development Committee has updated the course description and point distribution outline for the AP Psychology exam. Content review chapters in this test preparation book conform to their outline. The percentage range in front of each topic represents the number of questions about it that will be asked on the exam. For example, 8 to 10 questions will deal with Biological Bases of Behavior, and 7 to 9 questions will examine Learning.

10–14 percent	Scientific Foundations of Psychology
8–10 percent	Biological Bases of Behavior
6–8 percent	Sensation and Perception
7–9 percent	Learning
13–17 percent	Cognition
7–9 percent	Developmental Psychology
11–15 percent	Motivation, Emotion, and Personality
12–16 percent	Clinical Psychology
8–10 percent	Social Psychology

Typically free-response questions require you to make connections among concepts from multiple topics, or to apply concepts from different theoretical frameworks to design, analyze, or critique an experiment or other type of research study.

Who Grades My AP Psychology Exam?

The multiple-choice questions are scored by computer, but this is not possible for essay questions. These free-response questions are scored by a select group of experienced college professors of introductory psychology and AP Psychology teachers who gather at the

AP Reading for several days in June to assess the papers. Each of these faculty consultants spends a day or so getting trained on one question and one question only. Because each Reader becomes an expert on a single question and because each essay booklet is anonymous, this process provides a very consistent (**reliable**) and unbiased scoring of that question. During a typical day of grading, a random sample of each consultant's scored papers is selected and cross-checked by other experienced "Table Leaders" to ensure that consistency is maintained across all scorers throughout the Reading. The Reader's scores on a given question are also statistically analyzed to make sure that he or she is not giving scores that are significantly higher or lower than the mean scores given by other Readers of that question. All measures are taken to maintain consistency and fairness for your benefit. Your answers to the two questions will be scored by at least two different consultants.

AP Psychology exams are administered to college psychology students at the end of their introductory psychology course so that their performance on the AP Exam can be compared to their performance in the college course (as measured by their test and course grades). This information is used to guide the assignment of the AP exam grades 1 to 5 to raw scores.

Will My Exam Remain Anonymous?

Absolutely. Even if your high school teacher were to randomly rate one of your free-response questions at the Reading, there is virtually no way he or she would recognize that the paper belongs to you. To a faculty consultant, each student is a number, and to the computer, each student is a bar code.

What About That Permission Box on the Back?

The College Board uses some exams to help train high school teachers so that they can help the next generation of psychology students avoid common mistakes. If you check this box, you simply give permission to use your exam in this way. Even if you give permission, your anonymity is still maintained.

How Is My Multiple-Choice Answer Sheet Scored?

The multiple-choice section of the psychology exam is 100 questions and is worth two-thirds of your final score. Your answer sheet is run through the computer, which adds up your correct responses. The total number of right answers is your Section I Raw Score.

How Is My Free-Response Exam Scored?

Your performance on the free-response section is worth one-third of your final score. Two required essays compose this section. Although the two questions are typically given equal weight (25 each), they may be scored on different point scales. As a result, if Essay 1 has nine points that are scored, the number of points earned toward the total exam score for that essay would be Score 1×2.778. The multiplier for each free-response question is determined by dividing 25 by the maximum number of points in the scoring rubric or scoring guide. Table 1.2 indicates multipliers for essay questions with different point maximums.

Table 1.2 Points/Multiplier Table

Maximum Points	Multiplier
6	4.167
7	3.571
8	3.125
9	2.778
10	2.5
11	2.273
12	2.083

Section II Raw Score = (Score 1 × Correct Multiplier) + (Score 2 × Correct Multiplier)

So How Is My Final Grade Determined, and What Does It Mean?

To determine your Composite Raw Score, add the Section I Raw Score and the Section II Raw Score. Based on the composite scores of all the test takers, the Chief Reader sets four cut points that divide the composite scores into groups. Rather than report your composite score, the College Board reports to you one of five numbers assigned to your composite score based on the cut points:

- 5 indicates you are extremely well qualified.
- 4 indicates you are well qualified.
- 3 indicates you are qualified.
- 2 indicates you are possibly qualified.
- 1 indicates no recommendation.

Table 1.3 shows a rough example of a conversion chart, and as you complete the practice exams, you may use this to give yourself a hypothetical grade. Keep in mind that the conversion changes slightly every year to adjust for the difficulty of the questions. You should receive your grade in early July.

Table 1.3 Grade Guide Table—AP Psychology

Composite Score Range	AP Grade	Interpretation
104–150	5	Extremely Well Qualified for College Credit
90–103	4	Well Qualified
68–89	3	Qualified
50–67	2	Possibly Qualified
0–49	1	No Recommendation

Example

In Section I of Practice Exam 1, if you answered 76 questions correctly, your Section I score would be 76.

In Section II of Practice Exam 1, if you earned 7 out of 10 points on Essay 1 and 6 out of 8 points on Essay 2, your Section II score would be 36.25.

$$\text{Section II Raw Score} = (7 \times 2.5) + (6 \times 3.125)$$
$$= 17.5 + 18.75 = 36.25$$

Your composite score would be $76 + 36.25 = 112.25$, which would be assigned a 5.

What Should I Bring to the Exam?

On exam day, I suggest bringing the following items:

- Several pencils and an eraser that doesn't leave smudges.
- Black- or blue-colored pens for the free-response section.
- A watch so that you can monitor your time. You never know if the exam room will have a clock on the wall that keeps accurate time.
- Your school code.
- Your photo identification and social security number.
- Tissues.
- Your quiet confidence that you are prepared.

Avoid bringing electronic data and communications devices and study materials to the testing site.

How to Plan Your Time

IN THIS CHAPTER

Summary: The right preparation plan for you depends on your study habits, your own strengths and weaknesses, and the amount of time you have to prepare for the test. Take the diagnostic test in the next chapter to assess your strengths and weaknesses and get started.

Key Ideas

✪ Create a study plan that best suits your needs. It should consider your strengths and weaknesses, your study habits, and the amount of time you have to prepare for the AP Psychology exam.

✪ The first step in creating your study plan is to take the diagnostic test in the next chapter; it will help identify where you need to prioritize your review.

✪ Your study plan will depend on when you start your test preparation. You can choose a full school year, a one-semester, or a six-week timeline for your plan.

Your Personalized Study Plan for the AP Psychology Exam

Your study plan will be unique to your needs—your strengths and weaknesses and the amount of time you have to review. It's up to you to decide how you want to use this book to study for the AP Psychology exam. This book is designed for flexibility; you can work through it in order or skip around however you want. In fact, no two students who purchase this book will probably use it in exactly the same way.

The first step in developing your plan is to take the diagnostic exam in the next chapter. This is a practice exam that closely mirrors the actual exam. By taking the diagnostic test, you'll find out exactly what the exam is like, and you can plan realistically to prepare for it. The diagnostic test also tells you what you are reasonably good at and what things you need to practice. Identify your weaknesses and focus on these first.

Also helpful in identifying strengths and weaknesses are the chapter summary and the key ideas that begin each content review chapter. Use these to test yourself to determine if you need to carefully review the chapter or if your knowledge will allow you to skip it and move on to chapters that you need to study more completely.

Three Timelines for Preparing for the AP Psychology Exam

Besides your strengths and weaknesses, another factor to consider is the amount of time you have to prepare for the test. This includes not only how long you have before the exam but also the amount of time you have to devote to the review effort. For example, for students who are taking more than one AP course and have to divide their study time among many demands, it is especially important to prioritize the areas they need to review.

Following are three timelines for study plans based on how long you have before the test. Decide on a timeline for your study plan, and get started.

The School-Year Timeline

Choose this timeline if you like to take your time going through the material. Following this plan will allow you to practice your skills and develop your confidence gradually. You should go through the chapters in the book as you go through the units of your course. Take the diagnostic exam during Christmas break, the first practice exam during spring break, and the final practice exam a week before the actual exam. You will be able to see your progress!

This book is filled with explanatory material and practice exercises. Beginning to work through the chapters at the beginning of the school year will allow you to get to all the material in the book and maximize your preparation for the exam.

The One-Semester Timeline

Starting in the middle of the school year should give you ample time to review and prepare for the exam. Begin by taking the diagnostic exam in the next chapter; this will give you an idea of what the test is like. You'll get sense of how hard the test will be for you, how much time you need to devote to practice, and which type of questions or tasks you most need to work on. Then skip around in this book, prioritizing the chapters that you most need to review or that you find most difficult. Take the first practice exam during spring break and the final practice exam a week or a few days before you take the actual test.

The Six-Week Timeline

OK, maybe you procrastinated a bit too long. But this might not be a problem if you are doing well in your AP Psychology class. In fact, preparation for the exam is included in most AP classes, so you may be better prepared for the exam than you realize.

Start by taking the diagnostic test in the next chapter to find out what the actual test will be like and to identify the chapters you most need to review. With limited time, it is especially important to prioritize wisely the areas you need to review. If you found the practice test difficult, try to devote as much time as possible to reviewing the chapters you found most difficult, especially to the practice problems in these chapters. Save time to take the practice exams at the back of this book; take the final one a few days before you take the actual test. Even if you did well on the diagnostic test, you should take both practice exams; taking them will give you experience in pacing yourself within the time limits of the exam.

When to Take the Practice Exams

Most students should take the diagnostic test in Chapter 3 when they begin the test preparation. Taking the test will show you what the actual exam will be like, and based on your performance, you can identify your strong points as well as the weaknesses you'll need to focus on. Take the first practice exam at the end of this book during spring break or midway through your test preparation to measure your progress and see if your priorities should change. Take the final practice exam a week, or perhaps only a few days, before the actual test.

The practice tests are perhaps the most important part of this book. Taking them will accomplish all of the following:

- Give you practice with all the different types of questions you'll encounter on the AP Psychology exam
- Allow you to measure your progress and identify areas you need to focus on in your test preparation
- Allow you to practice pacing yourself with the time limits imposed on the test

Following are some things to remember as you plan your test preparation effort, regardless of when you start and how long you plan to practice:

- Establish a specific calendar of review so you stay on schedule and check off tasks as you complete them.
- Use your mobile phone to time yourself every time you take a timed test.
- Take advantage of the practice tests in this book. They are your friends.
- Don't stay up the night before the test trying to do some last-minute cramming; this may be counterproductive.

Good luck!

38. The greatest degree of resistance to extinction is typically found in which type of reinforcement schedule?

(A) continuous
(B) fixed ratio
(C) variable ratio
(D) fixed interval
(E) variable interval

39. In describing a ball that is both red and big, we say, "Big red ball," rather than "Red big ball," in the English language. Such a rule about word order is a specific rule of

(A) grammar
(B) syntax
(C) semantics
(D) spelling
(E) deep structure

40. Ralph thinks senior citizens are the ones who back up traffic on parkway entrance ramps because senior citizens are hesitant drivers. Every time he sees lots of cars waiting to enter the parkway, he looks to see who is driving the front car. If a senior citizen is in the driver's seat, he points it out to passengers in his car. Ralph is evidencing

(A) confirmation bias
(B) hindsight bias
(C) groupthink
(D) the availability heuristic
(E) the representativeness heuristic

41. Jho remembers which wavelengths of light are shorter than others by recalling ROYGBIV. ROYGBIV is an example of

(A) a mnemonic device
(B) the method of loci
(C) the self-reference effect
(D) constructive memory
(E) the representativeness heuristic

42. Knowing how to ride a bicycle is stored in which of our memory subsystems?

(A) explicit
(B) implicit
(C) semantic
(D) episodic
(E) declarative

43. Rather than taking the time to check the dictionary, Vinny used "*i* before *e*, except after *c*" to decide the spelling of "niether" (*sic*). To solve his spelling problem, Vinny applied

(A) Weber's law
(B) an algorithm
(C) the law of effect
(D) the misinformation effect
(E) a heuristic

44. After hearing this list of words, "Night, snore, bed, tired, pillow, dark, yawn, blanket, toss, turn," subjects were asked to write the words they heard. They frequently included the word *sleep*. This illustrates

(A) source amnesia
(B) procedural memory
(C) constructive memory
(D) retroactive interference
(E) proactive interference

45. When Sally moved to a new city, she didn't know where to find the spices she needed in the unfamiliar supermarket. As a result, Sally walked up and down each aisle until she located the spices in the same aisle as the baking supplies. The strategy Sally used to solve her problem best illustrates

(A) trial and error
(B) the availability heuristic
(C) representativeness heuristic
(D) an algorithm
(E) the belief perseverance

46. A phoneme is

(A) a set of rules for language
(B) a word or letter added to the end of another
(C) a word or letter placed before another
(D) the smallest meaningful unit of language
(E) the smallest distinctive sound unit of language

47. According to the drive reduction theory, the aim of drive reduction is

(A) raising motivation
(B) homeostasis
(C) incentive
(D) to maintain a tension state
(E) to increase arousal

GO ON TO THE NEXT PAGE

48. After Madison got home from the buffet (at which she stuffed herself), she went to the bathroom and made herself throw up. She does this every time she binges on food. She thinks about food a lot, craves chocolate, and would be considered of average weight. Madison is most likely suffering from

(A) anorexia nervosa
(B) bulimia nervosa
(C) set point depression
(D) panic disorder
(E) type A behavior

49. Physiological arousal, expressive behaviors, and conscious experience best characterize

(A) the two-factor theory
(B) motives
(C) incentives
(D) drives
(E) emotions

50. Physiological arousal is characterized by which of the following?

(A) contracted pupils and increased perspiration
(B) slowed digestion and accelerated heartbeat
(C) increased respiration and increased salivation
(D) contracted pupils and increased heartbeat
(E) dilated pupils and speeded digestion

51. Of the following, which means of communication is the most universal?

(A) English language
(B) hand gestures
(C) facial expressions
(D) vocal intonation
(E) bowing

52. After a portion of a rat's brain is destroyed, a scientist records dramatic weight gain in the rat. The portion of the rat's brain that was destroyed is most likely

(A) the hippocampus
(B) the hypothalamus
(C) the corpus callosum
(D) the angular gyrus
(E) Wernicke's area

53. As a race-car driver waits for the green flag to begin the race, his heartbeat increases and his mouth becomes dry. This is a result of increased

(A) amines
(B) serotonin
(C) cortisone
(D) adrenaline
(E) endorphins

54. Which of the following is an example of extrinsic motivation?

(A) dieting to become healthier
(B) going for a run because it relaxes you
(C) volunteering at the shelter to help others
(D) learning a new language because you find it interesting
(E) improving your golf score to earn more money while on tour

55. A person with X, X, and Y sex chromosomes must be

(A) heterosexual
(B) homosexual
(C) bisexual
(D) male
(E) female

56. According to Lev Vygotsky's sociocultural theory, the upper limit of a child's zone of proximal development is the level at which the child can

(A) solve a problem only with the help of a skilled instructor
(B) solve a difficult problem working alone
(C) recognize that the volume of a liquid stays the same whether it is in a tall, narrow container or a short, wide container
(D) use metacognitive skills to solve a problem
(E) perform logical deductions

57. Chemicals that cause birth defects are

(A) morphogenic
(B) homophobic
(C) homeostatic
(D) teratogenic
(E) pathogenic

58. Which controversy deals with the question of whether development is a gradual, cumulative change or a sequence of distinct stages?

(A) nature versus nurture
(B) continuity versus discontinuity
(C) stability versus change
(D) evolution versus creationism
(E) individualism versus collectivism

59. Darren is a happily married man who is a successful nursery school teacher. According to traditionalists, he has adopted the wrong

(A) gender
(B) gender identity
(C) gender role
(D) sex
(E) sexual orientation

60. The correct sequence of prenatal developmental stages is

(A) zygote, embryo, fetus
(B) embryo, fetus, zygote
(C) embryo, zygote, fetus
(D) zygote, fetus, embryo
(E) fetus, zygote, embryo

61. Frances, an 85-year-old retired teacher, feels that her life has been valued and she has made a positive impact on the lives of others. According to Erikson, Frances has achieved a sense of

(A) industry
(B) integrity
(C) generativity
(D) initiative
(E) autonomy

62. A marriage counselor can estimate a couple's marital satisfaction by the

(A) wife's positive attitude toward the marriage
(B) husband's experience in a prior marriage
(C) frequency of the couple's sexual activity
(D) ratio of their positive and negative interactions with each other
(E) all of the above

63. Freud's personality construct that contains psychic energy to power all personality systems and is guided by the pleasure principle is the

(A) id
(B) ego
(C) superego
(D) libido
(E) collective unconscious

64. After Rowena's boyfriend broke up with her, Rowena had a hot fudge sundae with four scoops of ice cream and whipped cream on top. Which defense mechanism does this exemplify?

(A) projection
(B) rationalization
(C) reaction formation
(D) regression
(E) displacement

65. Aurora enjoys playing with her young nieces and nephews because they always laugh and tell her how much fun she is. So Aurora goes out of her way to visit them. Her behavior is best explained by

(A) Sternberg's triarchic theory
(B) Gardner's multiple intelligences theory
(C) Hering's opponent process theory
(D) the halo effect
(E) Bandura's reciprocal determinism theory

66. Rolf is very reserved, is inner-directed, would rather be alone than with lots of people, rarely displays emotions, and is level-headed in an emergency. On Hans Eysenck's dimensions of personality, Rolf would be

(A) high on extroversion and high on psychoticism
(B) high on neuroticism and high on psychoticism
(C) high on extroversion and low on neuroticism
(D) low on extroversion and high on neuroticism
(E) low on extroversion and low on neuroticism

GO ON TO THE NEXT PAGE

67. Social–cognitive theorists would disagree with which of the following statements?

(A) a positive sense of self will help a person succeed in a new situation

(B) addressing conflicts in our unconscious can help resolve current challenges

(C) individuals with high self-esteem will be more successful at continuing work on a difficult task

(D) past performance can help predict a person's effectiveness in similar future circumstances

(E) observing police department trainees in simulated robberies can help determine a candidate's potential

68. The statement "A musician must make music; an artist must paint; a poet must write if he is to be ultimately at peace with himself" was most likely said by

(A) Sigmund Freud

(B) Carl Rogers

(C) Hans Eysenck

(D) Abraham Maslow

(E) Karen Horney

69. When two-year old Tyler loses his toy, he throws a temper tantrum and stomps his feet on the floor. According to Freud, the boy's tantrum is evidence that Tyler could not resist the demands of his

(A) id

(B) ego

(C) superego

(D) Oedipus complex

(E) Electra complex

70. The Rorschach inkblot test is

(A) a personality inventory

(B) used to fingerprint suspects

(C) an aptitude test

(D) an achievement test

(E) a projective personality test

71. In a normal distribution

(A) the range is always the same

(B) the standard deviation is equal to the range

(C) the standard deviation equals about 34 percent

(D) the median is equal to the mode

(E) the mean is equal to the standard deviation

72. Peter Salovey and John Mayer's concept of emotional intelligence is most similar to which of Howard Gardner's intelligences?

(A) analytic and practical

(B) naturalist and existential

(C) interpersonal and intrapersonal

(D) bodily/kinesthetic and verbal/linguistic

(E) spatial and logical

73. All good achievement tests should have
 I. content validity
 II. predictive validity
 III. reliability

(A) I only

(B) II only

(C) III only

(D) I and III only

(E) I, II, and III

74. All polar bears appear to have a white coat at birth. In warmer climates about 25 percent appear to have yellow or green coats as they age because of algae growing on them. The heritability of the white coat phenotype is

(A) 0 percent

(B) 25 percent

(C) 50 percent

(D) 75 percent

(E) 100 percent

75. According to Claude Steele, self-fulfilling prophecy might account for the poorer performance of African Americans on intelligence tests and girls on mathematics achievement tests because of

(A) generalized anxiety disorder

(B) stereotype threat

(C) neuroticism

(D) the primacy effect

(E) psychological profiling

76. A process used to identify clusters or groups of related items on a test is called

(A) correlation

(B) factor analysis

(C) normative curve

(D) experimental design

(E) controlled variable

77. Although your friend thinks there is nothing wrong with her, you are concerned with her behavior of unplugging every electrical item in her house every time she leaves, including all lamps, radios, the television, toaster, clocks, and telephones. Her behavior might be considered abnormal because

(A) she doesn't know right from wrong
(B) it is atypical and violates cultural norms
(C) she thinks it interferes with her everyday life
(D) it is insane
(E) it is dangerous

78. Which of the following perspectives attributes abnormal behavior to failure to resolve unconscious conflicts?

(A) biological
(B) behavioral
(C) psychoanalytic
(D) humanistic
(E) evolutionary

79. Narcissistic personality disorder is characterized by

(A) unwarranted suspiciousness and mistrust of other people
(B) a lack of interest in social relationships
(C) a grandiose sense of one's own importance
(D) instability revolving around problems of mood and thought processes
(E) pleasure-seeking, shallow feelings, lack of conscience

80. David thought he heard a dog telling him to kill people. Hearing the dog talking is an example of

(A) a hallucination
(B) a delusion
(C) inappropriate affect
(D) incoherent speech
(E) palsy

81. The intent of the *DSM-5* is chiefly to

(A) classify psychological disorders
(B) treat psychological disorders
(C) prevent physiological disorders
(D) cure psychological disorders
(E) create labels of physiological disorders

82. One common characteristic among many people with antisocial personality disorder is that they tend to

(A) be young women with connections to gang violence
(B) lack remorse or shame
(C) fall in love easily
(D) appear nervous and insecure
(E) suffer from a psychological disorder

83. Which of the following is a positive symptom of schizophrenia?

(A) catatonia
(B) reduced speech
(C) social withdrawal
(D) delusions
(E) flat affect

84. According to the *DSM-5*, OCD is classified as:

(A) an anxiety disorder
(B) a neurodevelopmental disorder
(C) obsessive-complusive and related disorder
(D) somatic disorder
(E) addictive disorder

85. The American Psychiatric Association's *DSM-5* (*Diagnostic and Statistical Manual of Mental Disorders*)

(A) is meant to be used by psychiatrists but not psychologists
(B) describes the causes of a variety of mental disorders
(C) explains why homosexuality should be considered a mental disorder
(D) contains case illustrations to help diagnosticians identify a client's disorder
(E) defines categories of mental disorders in terms of symptoms

86. Which is a behavioral therapy that has proved successful in treating phobias?

(A) electroconvulsive shock treatment
(B) group therapy
(C) psychosurgery
(D) systematic desensitization
(E) rational emotive therapy

GO ON TO THE NEXT PAGE

87. Psychoanalytic therapy and humanistic therapy differ in that psychoanalytic therapy focuses on

(A) the present and humanistic therapy focuses on the future

(B) subconscious and preconscious thoughts and humanistic therapy focuses on conscious thoughts

(C) curing illness and humanistic therapy focuses on preventing illness

(D) fixations and humanistic therapy focuses on insight

(E) probing past feelings and humanistic therapy focuses on exploring feelings as they occur

88. Clients who drink too much alcohol are sometimes treated with a drug that causes nausea if the client consumes alcohol. This type of therapy is known as

(A) systematic desensitization

(B) progressive relaxation

(C) client-centered therapy

(D) aversive conditioning

(E) psychodynamic therapy

89. Light therapy, consisting of exposure to bright light in the morning, has been successful in relieving symptoms of

(A) dissociative amnesia

(B) seasonal affective disorder

(C) schizophrenia

(D) obsessive-compulsive disorder

(E) Alzheimer's disease

90. Prozac, Zoloft, and Paxil help elevate mood by

(A) increasing the availability of serotonin to postsynaptic neurons

(B) decreasing the availability of norepinephrine to postsynaptic neurons

(C) facilitating reuptake of serotonin

(D) acting as agonists of dopamine

(E) preventing reuptake of dopamine

91. Which of the following would not occur in Aaron Beck's therapy for depression?

(A) gentle questions to reveal irrational thinking

(B) persuasion of the client to change his perception of his actions

(C) recognition of negative self-talk

(D) historical reconstruction, interpretation of resistance, and transference

(E) helping clients make more realistic appraisals

92. A college professor asked a biology teacher to let a college student observe her teaching for one period. After the student observed the teacher, the professor asked the teacher to accept the student as a student teacher for 10 weeks. She agreed. The strategy the professor used to get the teacher to agree is called

(A) cognitive dissonance

(B) foot-in-the-door phenomenon

(C) obedience to authority

(D) normative social influence

(E) conformity

93. As part of each lab, Ms. Geraci requires her students to wash their glassware so it is clean for the next class. She has found that the glassware is cleaner when students wash it in full view of their classmates. This is best explained by

(A) deindividuation

(B) the mere exposure effect

(C) social facilitation

(D) social loafing

(E) superordinate goals

94. In Heartsaver AED training, the American Heart Association teaches rescuers to direct specific people standing around the victim to do specific jobs, such as calling 911. Directing specific people to perform these jobs prevents

(A) the victim from dying

(B) people from feeling scared

(C) group polarization

(D) the bystander effect

(E) a social trap

The Diagnostic Exam

SECTION II

Time—50 minutes

Directions: Take approximately 50 minutes to answer both of the essay questions. According to the College Board directions, "It is not enough to answer a question by merely listing facts. You should present a cogent argument based on your critical analysis of the question posed, using appropriate psychological terminology." Write your essays on separate sheets of paper.

Essay 1:

[A] A study showed that after a car accident involving head trauma, many patients complain of similar symptoms. The most common of these symptoms are headache, dizziness, difficulty reading, and difficulty understanding what has been said to them. Discuss three possible areas of the brain that could be affected and why each affected area could cause the observed symptoms.

[B] Similar symptoms are found in employees of an industrial company. A researcher hired to analyze the symptoms believes a chemical, rather than head trauma, may be the cause. Design and describe a study the researcher could perform to test this hypothesis. In your description, you should include a description of how each of the following would apply to your study:

- Population
- Subject selection
- Illusory correlation
- Correlation coefficient
- Potential confounding variable
- Ethics

Essay 2:

Often misunderstood, autism spectrum disorder (ASD) is a psychological disorder affecting approximately 1.5 percent of the population. In addition to treating the disorder, psychologists work to identify its nature and origin, as well as help parents work with their affected child.

- Identify two characteristic symptoms used to diagnose ASD.
- Discuss two risk factors associated with the potential for ASD.
- Describe one medical treatment and identify a risk inherent in the use of this treatment in ASD.
- Describe one psychological treatment for ASD.
- People sometimes confuse ASD with attention deficit hyperactivity disorder (ADHD). Identify two characteristics that differentiate ADHD from autism spectrum disorder.

END OF DIAGNOSTIC EXAM

❯ Answers and Explanations, Section II

Essay 1
Scoring Rubric for Essay 1

This is a 9-point essay: 1 point for each of three areas of the brain affected by head trauma, including observed symptoms, and 1 point for a description of how each term in [B] applies to the study described.

Note: For all of part [A], responses should explain how each area of the brain plays a role in one of the symptoms mentioned in the essay. Three of the four symptoms must be explained.

Points 1–3: Explanation of source of headache, such as neuroinflammation and release of neurotransmitters.

(**Exception:** Stating the headache is caused by head trauma without identifying damage to brain.)

Explanation of source of *dizziness*, such as vestibular disruption of basilar membrane of inner ear or cerebellar damage.

Explanation of source of *difficulty reading*, such as injury to any region of the brain involved in the visual or comprehensive process of reading.

Explanation of source of *impaired auditory comprehension*, including Wernicke's area.

Points 4–9: Design an experiment.

- 1 point for **Population**—Target population is the entire group of individuals or employees in the industrial facility to which researchers are interested in generalizing their conclusions. The research population comprises the experimental and control groups, a smaller portion of the target population, through which generalizations can be made.
- 1 point for **Subject selection**—a subgroup of the target population to be selected at random so that each individual has an equal chance of being put in either the experimental or control group.
- 1 point for **Illusory correlation**—which occurs when an event appears to be related to the cause(s) of the symptoms but where in reality no relationship exists.
- 1 point for **Correlation coefficient**—a measure of how closely the symptoms displayed by the subjects are related to the presence of the chemical.
- 1 point for **Confounding variables**—those forces which may be at work to skew the experiment, such as fatigue, eye strain, cold/flu, etc., that may appear to present similar symptoms in the population.
- 1 point for **Ethics**—the essay must address appropriate experimental consideration of all subjects, following appropriate ethical guidelines.

Sample Essay

A traumatic brain injury can occur as a result of any force that penetrates or fractures the skull. Traumatic brain injury from a car accident may affect many parts of the brain. The likelihood is that the victim's head either struck the windshield or a side window or was jarred, resulting in a concussive force.

Post-traumatic headache may be caused by cellular injury which increases the concentration of extracellular potassium, triggering neuronal depolarization and the release of neurotransmitters that promote headaches. Neuroinflammation can be characterized by the activation of microglia and the release of proinflammatory chemicals, including chemokines. Dizziness may be caused by a vestibular disruption as a dysfunction of the basilar membrane of the semicircular canals of the inner ear, or a dysfunction of the part of the cerebellum that controls balance and equilibrium. A number of brain regions are involved in reading and comprehension. Broca's area in the frontal lobe controls the production of speech and language. The angular and supramarginal gyri link different parts of the brain so that letter shapes can be interpreted and combined to form words. The temporal lobe is responsible for phonological awareness for decoding and discriminating sounds. Damage to any one of these areas during a car accident will result in difficulty reading. Damage to the eyes, cornea, lens, or optic nerve might create visual disturbances which will also lead to difficulty reading. Damage to Wernicke's area located in the temporal lobe will result in a victim's inability to comprehend language, making it difficult to understand what others are saying.

To determine if a chemical were to cause similar symptoms in an industrial facility, a researcher would conduct an experiment in which sample employees would be divided into two groups, the research population. One group would be exposed to the chemical in question and the other would not, acting as the experimental and control groups, respectively. Since the target population, or the entire roster of employees, is probably too large to investigate, the researcher would select a portion of the employees as the experimental or research population. All employees of the company would have an equal chance of being selected for the experiment. The researcher might choose to use every fourth person who reports to work on a single day as the selection criteria. Random assignment would also be utilized to place participants into the experimental or control group. Random selection is essential to external validity, or the extent to which the researcher can use the results of the study to generalize to the larger population. Random assignment is necessary for internal validity, which allows the researcher to make causal claims about the effect of the chemical. Both the experimental and control groups would be given specific tasks to perform, such as reading a passage and responding to comprehension questions, assembling a puzzle, or other fine-motor skill tasks. The researcher will collect data based on scores, time for completion, and/or accuracy. The employees assigned to the experimental group would conduct their tasks while being exposed to the chemical in question. Those in the control group would work in an environment clean of any chemicals. Data on the results of the performance by two groups will be collected and compared.

The researcher should be aware of the potential for any illusory correlations, or those events that appear to be related in which, in fact, no relationship exists. The evidence may suggest that the presence of a particular chemical has caused the headaches, dizziness, and other symptoms, but it may be due to other factors. One can state that there is a particular chemical present in the industrial building and that many employees have headaches. To state that the chemical has caused the headaches requires experimental evidence. While presenting the data collected from the experiment, the correlation coefficient will indicate how closely the symptoms are related to the presence of the chemical. A strong relationship will have a coefficient value closer to 1.0. A negative correlation will indicate that as one variable increases, in this experiment it would be the level of chemical, the other variable, in this case the symptoms, would decrease. A positive correlation will indicate that as one variable increases, so does the other. A strong positive correlation with a high positive coefficient will indicate a strong relationship between the presence of the chemical and the employees' symptoms.

Confounding variables may pose a hurdle to the success of the researcher's efforts. An example of this may be employees having difficulty reading directions due to fatigue or eye strain in the workplace. Headaches may be caused by the prevalence of loud noises or poor lighting in the workplace rather than the chemical in question.

Any experiment using live subjects requires strict use of appropriate ethical guidelines. Subjects should be made aware of the purpose of the experiment and what they could expect to experience. This includes an understanding of the potential dangers that may arise as a result of exposure to the chemical in question. Long-term effects of this exposure might be unknown.

Essay 2
Scoring Rubric for Essay 2

This is a 9-point essay.

Points 1–2: **Two characteristic symptoms** of ASD can include any of the following: ongoing social problems; difficulty communicating and/or interacting with others; repetitive behaviors; limited interests or activities; manifestations that typically are recognized in the first two years of life; attributes that impede the individual's ability to function socially, at school or work, or in other life activities.

Points 3–4: **Two risk factors** may include gender, siblings with ASD, older parents at time of birth, and genetic conditions such as Down syndrome, fragile X syndrome, and tuberous sclerosis.

Points 5–6: **Medication and inherent risk period** Several medications are used to treat symptoms of ASD. Examples of the medications and associated risks are shown in the following table.

Medication	Risk
Risperidone (Risperdal)	Jerky, involuntary movements; anxiety; insomnia; muscle spasms
SSRIs	Increased suicidal thoughts, agitation or nervousness, dizziness, drowsiness
Tricyclics	Blurred vision, weight gain or loss, reduced blood pressure upon standing
Psychoactives or antipsychotics	Drowsiness, dizziness, restlessness, weight gain, tremors
Stimulants	Chest pain, high blood pressure, muscle weakness, rashes
Antianxiety medications	Increased risk of suicide in children, agitation or nervousness, dizziness, drowsiness
Anticonvulsants	Serious drop in the number of white blood cells and/or platelets, rashes, liver failure, anemia

Point 7: **Psychological treatment.** Early integrated developmental and behavioral interventions for ASD include family training, speech therapy, hearing impairment therapy, nutritional services, physical therapy, behavioral management therapy, cognitive therapy, joint attention therapy, and social skills training.

Points 8–9: Two characteristics that differentiate ADHD and ASD can include how the brain develops in ADHD and how children with ASD struggle to focus on things they dislike while those with ADHD lose interest and avoid focusing on things they dislike.

ASD	ADHD
Struggle to focus on things they dislike	Lose interest and avoid focus on things they need to concentrate on
Tend to be self-centered	May engage best with others and have difficulty remaining self-occupied
Have difficulty putting thoughts and feelings into words	Tend to talk non-stop, likely to interrupt, can talk at length about areas of interest
Love order and repetition	Do not like doing the same thing or the same thing for long periods
Find it hard to make eye contact	May not make eye contact while speaking

Sample Essay

Autism spectrum disorder is group of developmental disorders which encompass a wide range, or spectrum, of symptoms, levels of disability, and skills. The severity and characteristics of the symptoms can vary greatly from one individual to the next. The most common may include ongoing social problems, including difficulty communicating and interacting with others. Children with autism spectrum disorder find it difficult to make eye contact with others. They exhibit repetitive behaviors such as rocking, hand movements, and repetitive sounds or words. They display limited interests or activities, with intense focus on a singular item, theme, or color. Symptoms typically are recognized in the first two years of life and may impede the individual's ability to function socially, at school or work, or other areas of life.

Risk factors that may contribute to the likelihood of a child developing autism spectrum disorder include being born to older parents, typically a mother over 35 years and/ or father over 40 years. Research at the University of California, Davis, has shown that the risk of developing the disorder was higher if an older sibling has also been diagnosed with it. Younger male siblings were three times more likely to have autism than their female counterparts. About 20% of children with autism also have other genetic disorders such as Down syndrome or fragile X syndrome according to the National Institute of Mental Health.

No medication currently available can cure autism spectrum disorder, but there are a number of drugs that can treat certain symptoms, especially the behavioral ones. Most of these drugs, however, have their own list of side effects. One such medical treatment is the drug risperidone (Risperdal), which can suppress irritability in children between the ages of 5 and 16. It is often prescribed to treat schizophrenia and helps to rebalance the neurotransmitters dopamine and serotonin to improve thinking, mood, and behavior. Some people may develop muscle-related side effects such as tardive dyskinesia while taking risperidone. Symptoms include slow or jerky involuntary movements that cannot be controlled, often starting in the mouth with tongue rolling or chewing movements. Less risky side effects of taking Risperdal include anxiety, insomnia, and muscle spasms or tics.

The most effective psychological treatment for autism spectrum disorder includes early identification and early intervention, which is most likely to have positive effects on symptoms and skills as children grow. Because of the wide variety of symptoms, there can be a smorgasbord of treatments. One such treatment is cognitive behavioral therapy, which focuses on the connections between thoughts, feelings, and behaviors. The therapist, the person with the disorder, and his/her parents work together to create a therapeutic plan to booklet so that you can easily come back to it after you've finished all of the other questions. Be sure to skip the corresponding answer row on your answer sheet. You have an average of about 45 seconds to answer each question. Perhaps a question later in the exam will provide information or a retrieval cue that will enable you to answer the question you originally skipped. Go back to questions you skipped after doing all the other questions. Put your answers on the answer sheet.

6. Don't "overthink." Some of the questions may be easy for you to answer. Answer them and move on. Don't think that they are too easy. What is easy for you may be difficult for other people.

7. Yes, you absolutely should guess. Students who took the AP Psychology exam used to get penalized for wrong answers, but this is no longer the case. Because your Section I raw score equals the number of correct responses, you might improve your score by guessing on the questions you aren't sure of. You will probably have some idea about the concept being tested, so the odds are that you'll be able to eliminate at least some of the answer choices and improve your chances of guessing correctly. Even if you don't know anything about the concept and can't eliminate answer choices, you should still guess. You can't get any credit for an answer you leave blank, so don't leave any blanks on your answer sheet.

8. Change an answer only if you have a good reason for the change.

9. Time flies. Keep an eye on your watch as you pass the halfway point. If you are running out of time and you have a few questions left, skim them for the easy (and quick) ones so that the rest of your scarce time can be devoted to those that need a little extra reading or thought.

Other things to keep in mind:

- Take the extra half of a second required to clearly fill in the bubbles.
- Don't smudge anything with sloppy erasures. If your eraser is smudgy, ask the proctor for another.
- Absolutely, positively, check that you are bubbling the same line on the answer sheet as the question you are answering. I suggest that every time you turn the page you double-check that you are still lined up correctly.

Section II: The Free-Response Questions

Free-response questions on the AP Psychology exam may differ from the essay questions you've answered in other subjects. High interrater **reliability**, the extent to which two or more scorers evaluate the responses in the same way, is very important on the AP exam because you should get the same score no matter who reads your paper. Because only your own teacher ordinarily grades your classroom tests, this is not usually of importance. One aspect of ensuring high interrater reliability is by creating questions that have specific, correct answers that raters look for in scoring. The scoring guidelines are rubrics that are written and followed for each free-response question.

When approaching each FRQ, think of the acronym PEST. It stands for

- **Paragraph.** Always write in paragraph format; no bullet points or incomplete sentences.
- **Examples.** Always support your definition with *clear* examples that are comprehensible to the reader. Do not use examples like "the time in class when my teacher did . . ." Often the definition alone won't give you a point; you'll need an example or application to score the point.

- **Stay in order of the question.** If you don't know all the parts of the question, leave a space for the part(s) you aren't answering. This will enable the reader to follow your train of thought; you can still get a point if you miss naming a term but describe it. Your answer will be scored in the context of how the question was ordered.
- **Time.** Be aware of how much time you have for each question. Read both questions first and allocate approximately 22 minutes for each question. The 22 minutes should include a 5-minute window at the end to check your answer and add supporting evidence or make any final changes.

Although there are no magic pills to enable you to answer the free-response questions perfectly, let's look at some possible strategies for maximizing your score:

1. Read **both** essay questions to get a quick idea of the topics you'll need to recall. Directly jot down some key terms that serve as retrieval cues for you.

2. Note the time and allot about half the remaining minutes to each question. Stick to the time you've allotted for your first question so that you'll have adequate time to answer the second one.

3. Read the question again carefully. Underline or highlight key words. Say the question to yourself in your own words. Be sure you know what the question is asking. (If you are not sure, read the question again.)

4. See if you can segment the question into parts that will earn a credit. Generally, each question has 6 to 12 segments which each earn a credit. For example, if you are asked to differentiate between proactive and retroactive interference and give an example that illustrates each, you can segment the question into four points:
   Point 1—Define proactive interference.
   Point 2—Define retroactive interference, indicating clearly how it is different from proactive interference.
   Point 3—Give an example of proactive interference.
   Point 4—Give an example of retroactive interference.

5. No matter how much you write, you cannot get more than the one point allotted for any segment. Scorers look for an adequate answer for the point and move on. So should you!

6. No matter how brilliant an introduction you write, or what a great closing paragraph you create, if it doesn't answer a segment of the question, you will not earn credit for it. So, do NOT spend any time writing an introductory paragraph or a concluding paragraph. Do NOT spend time rewriting the question as an introductory statement. Start by answering the first question segment, and finish by answering the last question segment.

7. Write complete sentences. You cannot earn any points for a list or an outline. Unless you are specifically told that you can provide a graph, table, or diagram in your answer, you will NOT earn any credit for one.

8. Even if you are not sure of something that you think might possibly earn a credit, write it. You may get credit for it. Unless you are contradicting something else that you said, you will not have points subtracted for saying something wrong.

9. Write your answers clearly and legibly in dark blue or black ink. If you are equally comfortable printing or writing in script, print your answers. Readers appreciate easy-to-read answers. Put a line through anything you want to cross out. Do NOT waste time blackening out, erasing, or "whiting" out.

10. You don't need to get full credit in order to get a 5 on the AP exam. The better you do on the multiple-choice section, the more leeway you have for your essays.

"I was so 'time-tied' by the time I finished the first essay that if I hadn't scribbled some thoughts for the second question as soon as I got my paper, I'm sure I wouldn't have gotten that 5 on the exam!"
—Jessica, former AP student

"Vocabulary is the key to doing well. If you know the right terms, define them, and apply them to the question, you'll probably get most of the points. That's how I got a 5."
—Amanda, former AP student

STEP 4

Review the Knowledge You Need to Score High

CHAPTER 5

Scientific Foundations of Psychology

IN THIS CHAPTER

Summary: Psychology is the scientific study of behavior and mental processes. Behavior is anything you do that can be observed. Mental processes are your internal experiences such as thoughts, feelings, sensations, and perceptions. Scientific study involves systematic collection and examination of data (empirical evidence) to support or disprove hypotheses (predictions) rather than depending on common sense.

Psychology has a long past but a short history as a science. Although people have thought about their own behavior for thousands of years, the thinking was not done in an organized and scientific manner.

In their scientific study of behavior and mental processes, psychologists aim to describe, understand, predict, and explain psychological phenomena. **Theories** are organized sets of concepts that explain phenomena. Psychologists conduct research to answer behavioral questions. They systematically collect accurate data through a variety of carefully made observations and measurements. Scientific experiments, **naturalistic observations**, interviews, questionnaires, case studies, and psychological tests are some methods psychologists use to explore our personalities, values, intelligence, talents, and the effects of heredity and environment on our development. The scientific method is a set of general procedures psychologists use for gathering and interpreting data. Other researchers working independently must be able to obtain similar results using the same methods; this is called **replication**.

This chapter highlights the development of psychology as a science and the approaches, research methods, and statistics used to make sense of research data.

Key Ideas

- ✪ Roots of psychology are in philosophy and physiology/biology
- ✪ Structuralism and Functionalism—Schools of Psychology
- ✪ Behavioral approach
- ✪ Psychodynamic/psychoanalytic approach
- ✪ Humanistic approach
- ✪ Biological approach
- ✪ Evolutionary approach
- ✪ Cognitive approach
- ✪ Sociocultural approach
- ✪ Biopsychosocial model
- ✪ Domains of psychology
- ✪ Experimental method
- ✪ The controlled experiment
- ✪ Eliminating confounding variables
- ✪ Quasi-experimental research
- ✪ Correlational research
- ✪ Naturalistic observation
- ✪ Survey and test methods
- ✪ Case study
- ✪ Elementary statistics
- ✪ Descriptive statistics
- ✪ Measures of central tendency
- ✪ Measures of variability
- ✪ Correlation
- ✪ Graphic representation of correlation
- ✪ Inferential statistics
- ✪ Ethical guidelines

Roots of Psychology

Roots of psychology can be traced to philosophy and physiology/biology over 2,000 years ago in ancient Greece. As a result of examining organisms, physician/philosopher/physiologist Hippocrates thought the mind or soul resided in the brain but was not composed of physical substance (mind-body **dualism**). Philosopher Plato (circa 350 BC), who also believed in dualism, used self-examination of inner ideas and experiences to conclude that who we are and what we know are innate (inborn). On the other hand, Plato's student, Aristotle, believed that the mind/soul results from our anatomy and physiological processes (**monism**), that reality is best studied by observation, and that who we are and what we know are acquired from experience. About 2,000 years later (circa 1650), similar ideas persisted with René Descartes and John Locke. Descartes defended mind-body dualism (*Cogito ergo sum*—"I think, therefore I am") and that what we know is innate. On the other hand, empirical philosopher Locke believed that mind and body interact symmetrically (monism), knowledge comes from observation, and what we know comes from experience since we are born without knowledge, "a blank slate" (*tabula rasa*). The debate about the extent to which our behavior is inborn or learned through experience is called the **nature-nurture controversy.**

Schools of Psychology

"Knowing definitions is half the battle for a 5 [on the AP exam]."
—Jen, AP student

By the late 1800s, psychology was beginning to emerge as a separate scientific discipline. Biologist Charles Darwin applied the law of natural selection to human beings, forwarding the idea that human behavior and thinking are subject to scientific inquiry. Physiologists Ernst Weber and Gustav Fechner showed how physical events are related to sensation and perception. Hermann von Helmholtz measured the speed at which nerve impulses travel. Should their studies be considered under the heading of biology or psychology? There are many people and fields that will be explained in detail in the pages to come, please see the Table 5.1 for a summary reference of these.

Table 5.1 Leading Psychologists

Psychologist(s)	Description
Plato	Greek philosopher who argued for the role of nature in psychological development.
Aristotle	Greek philosopher who argued for the role of nurture in psychological development.
Thomas Hobbes	English philosopher.
René Descartes	French philosopher.
John Locke	English philosopher.
Jean-Jacques Rousseau	French philosopher.
Gustav Fechner	German experimental psychologist who deveoped the idea of the just noticeable difference (JND), which is considered to be the first empirical psychological measurement.
Charles Darwin	British naturalist whose theory of natural selection influenced the functionalist school and the field of evolutionary psychology.
Wilhelm Wundt	German psychologist who opened one of the first psychology laboratories and helped develop the field of structuralism.
Edward Bradford Titchener	American psychologist who contributed to the field of structuralism.
G. Stanley Hall	American psychologist who brought introspection to his lab at Johns Hopkins University in the United States; first president of the American Psychological Association.
Margaret Floy Washburn	First woman to complete her PhD in psychology.
William James	American psychologist who opened one of the first psychology laboratories and helped develop the field of functionalism.
Ivan Pavlov	Russian physiologist whose experiments on learning led to the principles of classical conditioning.
Hermann Ebbinghaus	German psychologist who studied the ability of people to remember lists of nonsense syllables under different conditions.
Sigmund Freud	Austrian psychologit who founded the field of psychodynamic psychology.
John B. Watson	American psychologist who contributed to the field of behaviorism.
Sir Frederic Bartlett	British psychologist who studied the cognitive and social processes of remembering.
Jean Plaget	Swiss psychologist who developed an important theory of cognitive development in children.
B. F. Skinner	American psychologist who contributed to the school of behaviorism.

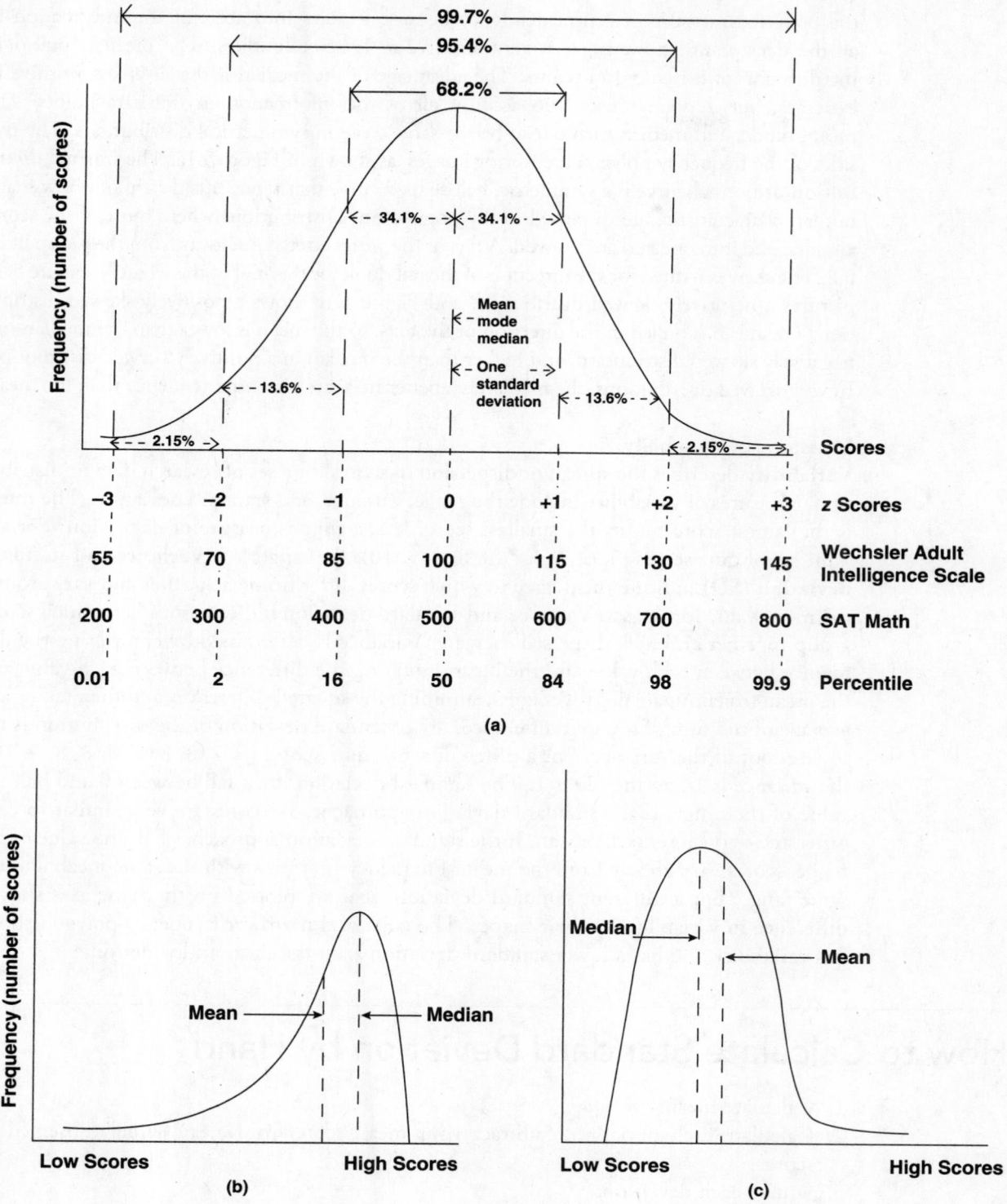

Figure 5.1 (a) The normal distribution or bell curve. (b) Negatively skewed distribution—skewed to the left. (c) Positively skewed distribution—skewed to the right.

the preferred measure of central tendency because it takes into account the information in all the data points; however, it is very sensitive to extremes/outliers. The mean is pulled in the direction of extreme data points. The advantage of the median is that it is less sensitive to extremes, but it doesn't take into account all of the information in the data points. The mean, mode, and median turn out to be the same score in symmetrical distributions. The two sides of the frequency polygon are mirror images, as shown in Figure 5.1a. The **normal distribution** or normal curve is a symmetric, bell-shaped curve that represents data about how many human characteristics are dispersed in the population. Distributions where most of the scores are squeezed into one end are **skewed.** A few of the scores stretch out away from the group like a tail. The skew is named for the direction of the tail (look for the "tail of the whate"). Figure 5.1b pictures a negatively skewed distribution, and Figure 5.1c shows a positively skewed distribution. The mean is pulled in the direction of the tails, so the mean is lower than the median in a negatively skewed distribution, and higher than the median in a positively skewed distribution. In very skewed distributions, the median is a better measure of central tendency than the mean.

Measures of Variability

Variability describes the spread or dispersion of scores for a set of research data or distribution. Measures of variability include the range, variance, and standard deviation. The **range** is the largest score minus the smallest score. It is a rough measure of dispersion. For the same set of quiz scores (5, 6, 7, 7, 7, 8, 8, 9, 9, 10), the range is 5. **Variance** and **standard deviation (SD)** indicate the degree to which scores differ from each other and vary around the mean value for the set. Variance and standard deviation indicate both how much scores group together and how dispersed they are. Variance is determined by computing the difference between each value and the mean, squaring the difference between each value and the mean (to eliminate negative signs), summing the squared differences and then taking the average of the sum of squared differences. The standard deviation of the distribution is the square root of the variance. For a different set of quiz scores (6, 7, 8, 8, 8, 8, 8, 8, 9, 10), the variance is 1 and the SD is 1. The standard deviation must fall between 0 and half the value of the range. If the standard deviation approaches 0, scores are very similar to each other and very close to the mean. If the standard deviation approaches half the value of the range, scores vary greatly from the mean. Frequency polygons with the same mean and the same range, but a different standard deviation, that are plotted on the same axes show a difference in variability by their shapes. The taller and narrower frequency polygon shows less variability and has a lower standard deviation than the short and wider one.

How to Calculate Standard Deviation by Hand

1. Calculate mean.
2. Calculate each deviation. Subtract your mean score from every actual (observed) score.
3. Square each deviation.
4. Find the "average" squared deviation by calculating the sum of the squared deviations divided by $(n - 1)$.
5. Divide that sum by the number of cases in your data.
6. Finally, calculate the square root of the number calculate in Step 4.

If you are not required to bring a calculator to the exam, you won't be required to figure out variance or standard deviation.

Correlation

Scores can be reported in different ways. One example is the **standard score** or **z score.** Standard scores enable psychologists to compare scores that are initially on different scales. For example, a z score of 1 for an IQ test might equal 115, while a z score of 1 for the SAT in mathematics might equal 600. The mean score of a distribution has a standard score of zero. A score that is one standard deviation above the mean has a z score of 1. A standard score is computed by subtracting the mean raw score of the distribution from the raw score of interest and then dividing the difference by the standard deviation of the distribution of raw scores. Another type of score, the **percentile score**, indicates the percentage of scores at or below a particular score. Thus, if you score at the 90th percentile, 90 percent of the scores are the same or below yours. Percentile scores vary from 1 to 99.

A statistical measure of the degree of relatedness or association between two sets of data, X and Y, is called the **correlation coefficient.** The correlation coefficient (r) varies from −1 to +1. One indicates a perfect relationship between the two sets of data. If the correlation coefficient is −1, that perfect relationship is indirect or inverse; as one variable increases, the other variable decreases. If the correlation coefficient (r) is +1, that perfect relationship is direct; as one variable increases, the other variable increases, and as one variable decreases, the other variable decreases. A correlation coefficient (r) of 0 indicates no relationship at all between the two variables. As the correlation coefficient approaches +1 or −1, the relationship between variables gets stronger. Correlation coefficients are useful because they enable psychologists to make predictions about Y when they know the value of X and the correlation coefficient. For example, if r = .9 for scores of students in an AP Biology class and for the same students in an AP Psychology class, a student who earns an A in biology probably earns an A in psychology, whereas a student who earns a D in biology probably earns a D in psychology. If r = .1 for scores of students in an English class and scores of the same students in an AP Calculus class, knowing the English grade doesn't help predict the AP Calculus grade.

Correlation does not imply causation. Correlation indicates only that there is *a relationship between variables, not how the relationship came about.*

The strength and direction of correlations can be illustrated graphically in **scattergrams** or **scatterplots** in which paired X and Y scores for each subject are plotted as single points on a graph. The slope of a line that best fits the pattern of points suggests the degree and direction of the relationship between the two variables. The slope of the line for a perfect positive correlation is r = +1, as shown in Figure 5.2a. The slope of the line for a perfect negative correlation is r = −1, as shown in Figure 5.2b. Where dots are scattered all over the plot and no appropriate line can be drawn, r = 0 as shown in Figure 5.2c, which indicates no relationship between the two sets of data.

(a)   (b)   (c)

Figure 5.2 (a) Scattergram for perfect positive correlation (r = +1.0). (b) Scattergram for perfect negative correlation (r = −1.0). (c) Scattergram for no relationship between two sets of data (r = 0).

Inferential Statistics

Inferential statistics are used to interpret data and draw conclusions. They tell psychologists whether or not they can generalize from the chosen sample to the whole population, if the sample actually represents the population. Inferential statistics use rules to evaluate the probability that a correlation or a difference between groups reflects a real relationship and not just the operation of chance factors on the particular sample that was chosen for study. **Statistical significance (p)** is a measure of the likelihood that the difference between groups results from a real difference between the two groups rather than from chance alone. Results are likely to be statistically significant when there is a large difference between the means of the two frequency distributions, when their standard deviations are small, and when the samples are large. Some psychologists consider that results are significantly different only if the results have less than a 1 in 20 probability of being caused by chance ($p < .05$). Others consider that results are significantly different only if the results have less than a 1 in 100 probability of being caused by chance ($p < .01$). The lower the p value, the less likely the results were due to chance. Results of research that are statistically significant may be practically important or trivial. Statistical significance does not imply that findings are really important. **Meta-analysis** provides a way of statistically combining the results of individual research studies to reach an overall conclusion. Scientific conclusions are always tentative and open to change should better data come along. Good psychological research gives us an opportunity to learn the truth.

Ethical Guidelines

Whether involved in research or practice, psychologists need to act responsibly and morally. Studies conducted by Harry Harlow involving rhesus monkeys separated from their mothers and subjected to frightening conditions, studies by Phil Zimbardo involving students role-playing prisoners and guards, and studies conducted by Stanley Milgram in which participants believed they were delivering painful electric shocks to another person were highly publicized in the 1960s and 1970s. Following Milgram's experiments, members of the American Psychological Association strengthened their ethical guidelines regarding research design, implementation, and practice; and other groups adopted similar guidelines. The guidelines prevent unnecessary deception and pain to humans and other animals, and they protect confidentiality.

All public and most private institutions have Institutional Review Boards (IRBs) that must approve all research conducted within their institutions. Boards specifically protect participants by requiring researchers to obtain signed informed-consent agreements from all participants. These statements describe procedures, risks, benefits, and the right of the participant not to participate or to withdraw from the research study without penalty at any time. Research participants cannot be deceived about significant aspects that would affect their willingness to participate. After the participant finishes his or her part or research is completed, participants are debriefed about the research (i.e., the nature, results, and conclusions of the research are revealed).

Psychologists who conduct research involving other animals must treat them humanely; acquire, care for, use, and dispose of animals properly; and make efforts to minimize their discomfort, infection, illness, and pain.

ary model (triune brain), the human brain has three major divisions, overlapping layers with the most recent neural systems nearest the front and top. The reptilian brain, which maintains homeostasis and instinctive behaviors, roughly corresponds to the brainstem, which includes the medulla, pons, and cerebellum. Developmental psychologists call the brainstem the hindbrain. The old mammalian brain roughly corresponds to the limbic system that includes the septum, hippocampus, amygdala, cingulate cortex, hypothalamus, and the thalamus, which are all important in controlling emotional behavior, some aspects of memory, and vision. The new mammalian brain or neocortex, synonymous with the cerebral cortex, accounts for about 80 percent of brain volume and is associated with the higher functions of judgment, decision making, abstract thought, foresight, hindsight and insight, language, and computing, as well as sensation and perception. Developmental psychologists call the structures of the "mammalian brain" the forebrain. The surface of your cortex has peaks called **gyri** and valleys called **sulci,** which form **convolutions** that increase the surface area of your cortex. Deeper valleys are called fissures. The last evolutionary development of the brain is the localization of functions on different sides of your brain.

Localization and Lateralization of the Brain's Function

Although multiple representations of information can be located within different areas of your brain, specific regions of your brain seem most critical in handling particular functions. This localization of structure and function has been identified for numerous regions (see Figure 6.1). **Association areas** are regions of the cerebral cortex that do not have

Figure 6.1   Major structures of the brain in medial view.

specific sensory or motor functions but are involved in higher mental functions, such as thinking, planning, remembering, and communicating. In general, the crossing over of nerves sending information from one side of your body to the other side of your brain results in **contralaterality,** control of one side of your body by the other side of your brain.

Structure of Brain	Function
MEDULLA OBLONGATA	Where most fibers cross, resulting in contralateral (opposite side) control. Regulates heart rhythm, blood flow, breathing rate, digestion, vomiting.
PONS	Includes portion of reticular activating system (a.k.a. reticular formation) critical for arousal. Bridge between cerebral hemispheres and both medulla and cerebellum.
CEREBELLUM	Coordinates motor function, integrating motion and positional information from the inner ear and muscles. Helps maintain balance.
BASIL GANGLIA (or basal nuclei)	Links the thalamus with the motor cortex and other motor areas. Regulates initiation of movements, balance, eye movements, and posture. Involved in reward/punishment learning, focus, and functions in processing of implicit memory. Some nuclei (neural clusters) involved in emotion.
THALAMUS	Relay "station" for sensory pathways carrying visual, auditory, taste, somatosensory information to/from appropriate areas of cerebral cortex. Some nuclei (neural clusters) involved in emotion.
HYPOTHALAMUS	Controls autonomic functions such as body temperature and heart rate via control of sympathetic and parasympathetic centers in the medulla. Sets appetitive drives (such as thirst, hunger, sexual desire) and behaviors. Sets emotional states, such as rage, with the limbic system. Integrates with endocrine system by secretion of hormones that regulate hormones from pituitary. Helps determine biological rhythms, such as the menstrual cycle.
AMYGDALA	Influences aggression and fear. Coordinates fight-or-flight response. Important in formation of sensory memory.
HIPPOCAMPUS	Enables formation of new long-term memories.
CEREBRAL CORTEX	Receives and processes sensory information and directs movement. Center for higher-order processes such as thinking, planning, judgment.

"To help remember that the hippocampus aides in the formation of new long-term memories, just remember that 'hippos are like elephants and elephants never forget.' Hippos = hippocampus = memory formation."
—Sarah B, AP student

Just as a map or globe can be divided into hemispheres and continents, your cerebral cortex can be divided into eight lobes, four in the left cerebral hemisphere and four in the right cerebral hemisphere (see Figure 6.2). Go to http://www.g2conline.org and click on 3-D Brain for a more detailed view of a three-dimensional brain model. You can download it as an app.

Region of Brain	Function
OCCIPITAL LOBES	Information from left half of visual field of both eyes is processed in right occipital lobe, from right visual field in left occipital lobe.
PARIETAL LOBES	Somatosensory cortex (for touch sensations) is the front strip. Contralateral representation of all body parts.
FRONTAL LOBES	Motor cortex strip just in front of somatosensory cortex initiates movements and integrates activities of skeletal muscles. Contralateral—right/left hemisphere controls other side of body. **Broca's area** in left frontal lobe controls production of speech. Interpret and control emotional behaviors, make decisions, carry out plans.
TEMPORAL LOBES	Center for hearing. **Wernicke's area** in left temporal lobe plays role in understanding language and making meaningful sentences. Right temporal lobe important for understanding music/tonality. Sound from both ears processed mostly contralaterally. Smell processed near front of temporal lobes.

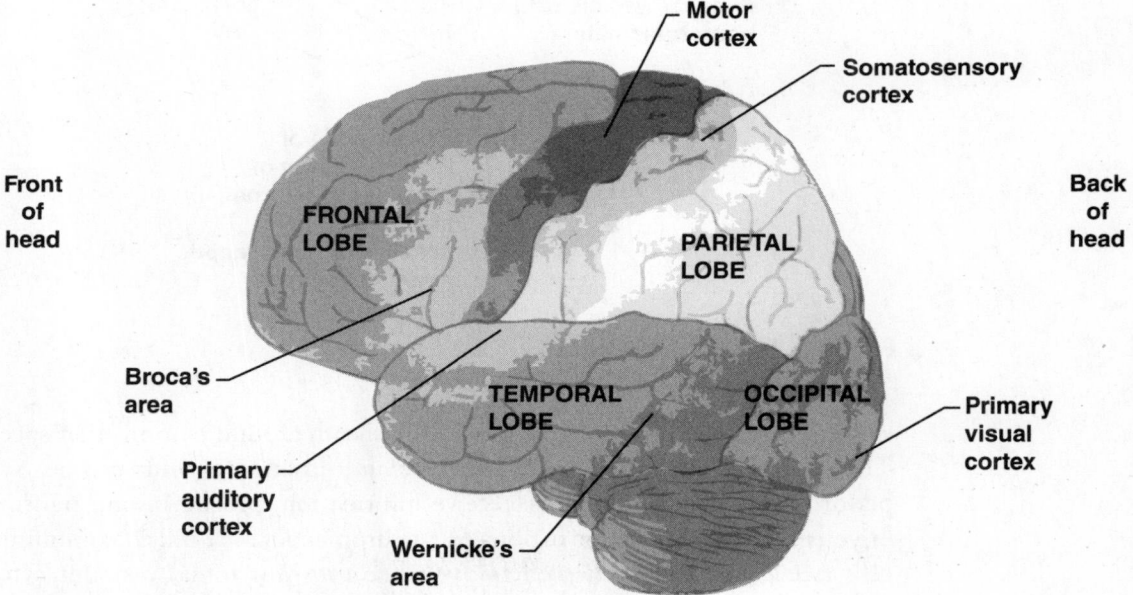

Figure 6.2   Regions of the left cerebral cortex in lateral view.

Although specific regions of the brain are associated with specific functions, if one region is damaged, the brain can reorganize to take over its function, which is called **plasticity.** In phantom limb syndrome, a somewhat unfortunate example of plasticity, reorganization of the somatosensory cortex leads to someone experiencing sensations where a missing limb used to be.

Structure and Function of the Neuron

Your extraordinarily complex brain is composed of trillions of neurons and glial cells. **Glial cells** guide the growth of developing neurons, help provide nutrition for and get rid of

Figure 6.3 Typical neurons.

wastes of **neurons,** and form an insulating sheath around neurons that speeds conduction. The neuron is the basic unit of structure and function of your nervous system. Neurons perform three major functions: receive information, process it, and transmit it to the rest of your body. Three major regions of a neuron enable the cell to communicate with other cells (see Figure 6.3). The **cell body** (a.k.a. cyton or soma) contains cytoplasm and the nucleus, which directs synthesis of such substances as neurotransmitters. The **dendrites** are branching tubular processes capable of receiving information. The **axon** emerges from the cyton as a single conducting fiber (longer than a dendrite) that branches and ends in tips called **terminal buttons,** axon terminals, or synaptic knobs. The axon is usually covered by an insulating **myelin sheath** (formed by glial cells). **Neurogenesis,** the growth of new neurons, takes place throughout life.

Neurotransmitters are chemicals stored in structures of the terminal buttons called synaptic vesicles. Different neurotransmitters have different chemical structures and perform different functions. For example, **acetylcholine (ACh)** causes contraction of skeletal muscles, helps regulate heart muscles, is involved in memory, and transmits messages between the brain and spinal cord. A lack of ACh is associated with Alzheimer's disease. **Dopamine** stimulates the hypothalamus to synthesize hormones and affects alertness and movement. A lack of dopamine is associated with Parkinson's disease; too much dopamine is associated with schizophrenia. **Glutamate** is a major excitatory neurotransmitter involved in information processing throughout the cortex and especially memory formation in the hippocampus. Both schizophrenia and Alzheimer's may involve glutamate receptors. **Serotonin** is associated with sexual activity, concentration and attention, moods, and emotions. A lack of serotonin is associated with depression. Opioid peptides such as **endorphins** are often considered the brain's own painkillers. **Gamma-aminobutyric acid (GABA)** inhibits firing of neurons. Benzodiazepine (Valium) and anticonvulsant drugs increase activity of GABA. Huntington's disease is associated with insufficient GABA-producing neurons in parts of the brain involved in coordination of movement. Seizures are associated with malfunctioning GABA systems. **Norepinephrine**, also known as noradrenaline, is associated with attentiveness, sleeping, dreaming, and learning. It is also released as a hormone into the blood where it contracts blood vessels and increases heart rate. Other chemicals, such as drugs, can interfere with the action of neurotransmitters. *Agonists* may mimic a neurotransmitter and bind to its receptor site to produce the effect of the neurotransmitter. *Antagonists* block a receptor site, inhibiting the effect of the neurotransmitter or agonist.

Neurotransmitters

Neurotransmitter	Function	Associations
Acetylcholine (Ach)	Learning, memory, muscle action	Too little acetylcholine is associated with Alzheimer's disease
Dopamine	Movement, learning, attention, and emotion	Too much dopamine is associated with schizophrenia Too little dopamine is associated with Parkinson's disease
Serotonin	Mood, hunger, sleep, and arousal	Too little serotonin is associated with depression
Norepinephrine	Alertness and arousal	Too little norepinephrine can depress mood
GABA	Inhibitory neurotransmitter	Too little GABA is linked to seizures and insomnia
Glutamate	Major excitatory neurotransmitter Involved with memory	Too much glutamate is associated with migraines and seizures

Neuron Functions

All your behavior begins with the actions of your neurons. A neuron receives incoming information from its receptors spread around its dendrites. That information is sent to its cell body, where it's combined with other incoming information. Neural impulses are electrical in nature along the neuron. The neuron at rest is more negative inside the **cell membrane** relative to outside of the membrane. The neuron's **resting potential** results from the selective permeability of its membrane and the presence of electrically charged particles called ions near the inside and outside surfaces of the membrane in different concentrations. When sufficiently stimulated (to threshold), a net flow of sodium ions into the cell causes a rapid change in potential across the membrane, known as the **action potential** (see Figure 6.4). If stimulation is not strong enough, your neuron doesn't fire. The strength of the action potential is constant whenever it occurs. This is the **all-or-none principle.**

Figure 6.4 Action potential.

The wave of **depolarization** and **repolarization** is passed along the axon to the terminal buttons, which release neurotransmitters. Spaces between segments of myelin are called nodes of Ranvier. When the axon is myelinated, conduction speed is increased since depolarizations jump from node to node. This is called **saltatory conduction.** Chemical neurotransmitters are released into the **synapse** where they attach to specific receptor sites on membranes of dendrites of your postsynaptic neurons, like a key fitting into the tumbler of a lock (the lock-and-key concept). Some of your synapses are **excitatory,** the neurotransmitters cause the neuron on the other side of the synapse to generate an action potential (to fire); other synapses are **inhibitory,** reducing or preventing neural impulses. The sum of all excitatory and inhibitory inputs determines whether your next neuron will fire and at what rate. The constant flow of these neurochemical impulses gives your behavior its amazing complexity. It regulates your metabolism, temperature, and respiration. It also enables you to learn, remember, and decide.

Reflex Action

The simplest form of your behavior, called a **reflex,** involves impulse conduction over a few (perhaps three) neurons. The path is called a **reflex arc.** Sensory or **afferent neurons** transmit impulses from your **sensory receptors** to the spinal cord or brain. **Interneurons,** located entirely within your brain and spinal cord, intervene between sensory and motor neurons. Motor or **efferent neurons** transmit impulses from your sensory or interneurons to muscle cells that contract or gland cells that secrete. Muscle and gland cells are called **effectors.** Examples of your reflexes include your pupillary reflex, knee jerk, sneezing, and blinking. Neural impulses travel one way along the neuron from dendrites to axons to terminal buttons and among neurons from the receptor to the effector.

The Endocrine System

Your endocrine system interacts with your nervous system to regulate your behavior and body functions. Your **endocrine system** consists of glands that secrete chemical messengers called **hormones** into your blood. The hormones travel to target organs where they bind to specific receptors. Endocrine glands include the pineal gland, hypothalamus, and pituitary gland in your brain; the thyroid and parathyroids in your neck; the adrenal glands atop your kidneys; pancreas near your stomach; and either testes or ovaries.

Endocrine Gland	Function
PINEAL GLAND	Produces melatonin that helps regulate **circadian rhythms** and is associated with **seasonal affective disorder.**
HYPOTHALAMUS	Produces hormones that stimulate or inhibit secretion of hormones by the pituitary.
PITUITARY GLAND	Sometimes called "master gland" because it produces stimulating hormones that promote secretion by other glands including: TSH—thyroid-stimulating hormone ACTH—adrenocorticotropic hormone stimulates adrenal cortex FSH—follicle stimulating hormone stimulates egg or sperm production Produces ADH (antidiuretic hormone) to help retain water in your body and HGH (human growth hormone).
THYROID GLAND	Produces thyroxine, which stimulates and maintains metabolic activities. Lack of thyroxine in children can result in mental retardation.
PARATHYROIDS	Produce parathyroid hormone that helps maintain the calcium ion level in blood that is necessary for normal functioning of neurons.
ADRENAL GLANDS	Adrenal cortex, the outer layer, produces steroid hormones such as cortisol, which is a stress hormone. Adrenal medulla, the core, secretes adrenaline (epinephrine) and noradrenaline (norepinephrine), which prepare the body for "fight or flight," like the sympathetic nervous system.
PANCREAS	Insulin and glucagon regulate blood sugar that fuels all behavioral processes. Imbalances result in diabetes and hypoglycemia, respectively.
OVARIES AND TESTES	Gonads in females and males, respectively, necessary for reproduction and development of secondary sex characteristics.

Genetics and Evolutionary Psychology

Why do you behave the way you do? To what extent is your behavior determined by your heredity? To what extent is it determined by your life history or environment? The **nature-nurture controversy** deals with the extent to which heredity and the environment each influence behavior. **Evolutionary psychologists** study how natural selection favored behaviors that contributed to survival and the spread of our ancestors' genes and may currently

› Review Questions

1. A neuron without terminal buttons would be unable to
   (A) receive information from neighboring neurons
   (B) generate an action potential
   (C) direct the synthesis of neurotransmitters
   (D) secrete neurotransmitters to postsynaptic neurons
   (E) transport ions across the cell membrane

2. Paul Broca found that the loss of the ability to speak intelligibly is associated with damage to a region of the brain in the
   (A) thalamus
   (B) right parietal lobe
   (C) right occipital lobe
   (D) left temporal lobe
   (E) left frontal lobe

3. Scientists are able to see changes in the brain as it processes information by means of
   (A) lesioning
   (B) autopsy
   (C) CT
   (D) MRI
   (E) PET

4. The simplest behaviors
   (A) are learned when we are infants
   (B) do not involve the central nervous system
   (C) are called instincts
   (D) include sneezing and blinking
   (E) must be processed by the medulla

5. Of the following, the effect of adrenaline on the body is most similar to the effect of the
   (A) cerebellum
   (B) parathyroids
   (C) somatic nervous system
   (D) parasympathetic nervous system
   (E) sympathetic nervous system

6. Mr. Jenkins suffered a "stroke" as a result of a brain injury. Although he can still move the fingers on his right hand, he has lost sensation in these parts. Of the following, the site of damage to his brain is most likely in the
   (A) right frontal lobe
   (B) right temporal lobe
   (C) left frontal lobe
   (D) left parietal lobe
   (E) hypothalamus

7. Of the following, which are located exclusively in the central nervous system?
   (A) afferent neurons
   (B) interneurons
   (C) efferent neurons
   (D) glial cells
   (E) effectors

8. Which of the following glands interact(s) most directly with all of the others to help regulate body processes?
   (A) pituitary
   (B) adrenals
   (C) parathyroids
   (D) thyroid
   (E) ovaries

9. Gunshot wounds, tumors, and strokes all result in
   (A) infections
   (B) significant loss of function
   (C) lesions
   (D) pain
   (E) necessity for surgery

10. Which of the following must be males?
    (A) dizygotic twins
    (B) monozygotic twins
    (C) Down syndrome children
    (D) Klinefelter's syndrome children
    (E) Turner syndrome children

11. Which includes all of the others?
    (A) autonomic nervous system
    (B) peripheral nervous system
    (C) somatic nervous system
    (D) parasympathetic nervous system
    (E) sympathetic nervous system

12. Which stimulate a muscle to contract?
    (A) adrenal hormones
    (B) receptors
    (C) sensory neurons
    (D) motor neurons
    (E) interneurons

13. The part of the brain most closely associated with maintaining balance and the coordination of complex sequences of movements is the
    (A) hypothalamus
    (B) thalamus
    (C) pons
    (D) medulla
    (E) cerebellum

14. A loss of the ability of the brain to produce adequate levels of dopamine often leads to
(A) aphasia
(B) Alzheimer's disease
(C) Parkinson's disease
(D) bipolar disorder
(E) amnesia

15. Which task is primarily a right cerebral hemisphere function in most people?
(A) understanding written language
(B) understanding spoken language
(C) processing visual information from the left eye
(D) recognizing faces
(E) processing sensory information from the right leg

16. As you are reading this question, you are probably not thinking about what you ate for lunch. The memory of what you ate for lunch is most likely in your
(A) nonconscious
(B) preconscious
(C) unconsciousness
(D) sensory memory
(E) attention

17. Traveling in a jet plane from California to New York is most likely to
(A) disrupt your circadian rhythms
(B) prevent the onset of REM sleep
(C) stimulate your parasympathetic nervous system
(D) induce delta brain waves
(E) cause withdrawal symptoms

18. According to psychodynamic psychologists, the unconscious
(A) processes information of which you are unaware
(B) includes unacceptable feelings, wishes, and thoughts
(C) is characterized by loss of responsiveness to the environment
(D) is synonymous with the preconscious
(E) develops after the ego and superego

19. Nightmares most frequently occur during
(A) NREM-1
(B) NREM-2
(C) NREM-3
(D) hypnagogic
(E) REM

20. During paradoxical sleep, muscles seem paralyzed and
(A) eyes dart about in various directions
(B) breathing is slow and shallow
(C) night terrors are likely
(D) sleepwalking occurs
(E) the sleeper is easily awakened

21. After her bridal shower, a young woman dreamed that she was dining with her parents when a young man grabbed her wallet containing her driver's license, credit cards, cash, and family pictures. She awoke in a cold sweat. After discussing the dream with a friend, she realized that she felt anxious about losing her identity in her approaching marriage. This explanation of her dream represents the
(A) manifest content
(B) latent content
(C) ego
(D) activation-synthesis theory
(E) cognitive analysis

22. Zen Buddhists and others practicing meditation are better able than most other people to stimulate their
(A) sympathetic nervous systems
(B) parasympathetic nervous systems
(C) somatic nervous systems
(D) salivation
(E) urination

23. Of the following, which pair of psychoactive drugs shares the most similar effects on the brain?
(A) alcohol–marijuana
(B) caffeine–morphine
(C) nicotine–heroin
(D) amphetamines–cocaine
(E) barbiturates–LSD

24. In small quantities, alcohol can be mistaken for a stimulant because it
(A) inhibits control of emotions
(B) stimulates the sympathetic nervous system
(C) speeds up respiration and heartbeat
(D) induces sleep
(E) affects the cerebellum

› Answers and Explanations

1. **D**—Terminal buttons secrete neurotransmitters into the synapse.

2. **E**—Broca's area is a region in the left frontal lobe anterior to the motor cortex.

3. **E**—PET scans visualize changes in the brain as it functions. While fMRI also shows changes in the brain as it functions, MRI and CT scans show structure only.

4. **D**—Our simplest behaviors are reflexes. Sneezing and blinking are reflexes.

5. **E**—Adrenaline is a hormone that speeds up breathing and heart rate, sends a message to change stored food back to glucose, etc. The sympathetic nervous system stimulates the same changes in the body.

6. **D**—The center for sensation in the brain is the somatosensory region of the cerebral cortex located in the front of the parietal lobes. Nerves carrying sensations from the right side of the body cross over to the left side of the brain, so the most probable site of damage is the left parietal lobe.

7. **B**—Interneurons are found in the brain and spinal cord only. The others can be found in the peripheral nervous system.

8. **A**—The pituitary gland, which is sometimes called "the master gland," produces many hormones that stimulate other glands, including the adrenals, parathyroids, thyroid, and ovaries.

9. **C**—Lesions are interruptions in tissue. While the other choices may accompany wounds, tumors, and strokes, they also may not.

10. **D**—Presence of the Y chromosome determines the sex of a human baby. Of the choices, only a Klinefelter's child (XXY) must have a Y chromosome.

11. **B**—The peripheral nervous system comprises the autonomic nervous and somatic nervous system. The autonomic nervous system is subdivided into the parasympathetic and sympathetic nervous systems.

12. **D**—Motor neurons or efferent neurons cause muscles to contract or glands to secrete.

13. **E**—The cerebellum functions in balance and coordination.

14. **C**—Parkinson's disease is associated with depletion of cells that produce dopamine.

15. **D**—Pattern matching and picture and facial recognition are all right hemispheric functions.

16. **B**—Memories that can easily be brought into consciousness are in the preconscious level of consciousness.

17. **A**—Crossing time zones can change the amount of light and dark your body gets and alter your sleeping/waking cycle, secretion of hormones, etc. This disrupts your circadian rhythms.

18. **B**—According to psychoanalysts/psychodynamic psychologists, the unconscious harbors unacceptable thoughts, wishes, and feelings that can be revealed in dreams, through hypnosis, etc.

19. **E**—Nightmares are unpleasant, complex dreams that occur mainly during REM sleep.

20. **A**—A paradox is something contradictory that is true. REM sleep is considered paradoxical sleep because the eyes are darting around, brain waves are similar to being awake, but the muscles of the arms and legs are inactive.

21. **B**—Freudians believe the hidden meaning of a dream is its latent content.

22. **B**—Ordinarily we lack the ability to activate our parasympathetic nervous systems to any significant extent, but we can easily activate the other functions listed.

23. **D**—Amphetamines and cocaine are both classified as stimulants.

24. **A**—After drinking small amounts of alcohol, people are often lively and seem uninhibited. This results from inhibition of part of the frontal lobes that usually keep emotions in check.

› Rapid Review

Neuropsychologists—those who explore the relationships between brain/nervous systems and behavior. Neuropsychologists are also called biological psychologists or biopsychologists, behavioral geneticists, physiological psychologists, and behavioral neuroscientists.

Studying patients with brain damage linked loss of structure with loss of function.

Lesions—precise destruction of brain tissue, enables more systematic study of the loss of function resulting from surgical removal (also called ablation), cutting of neural connections, or destruction by chemical applications.

CT scans and MRIs show structure.

- **Computerized axial tomography (CAT or CT)**—creates a computerized image using X-rays passed through the brain to show structure and/or the extent of a lesion.

- **Magnetic resonance imaging (MRI)**—creates more detailed computerized images using a magnetic field and pulses of radio waves that cause emission of signals that depend upon the density of tissue.

EEGs, PET scans, and fMRIs show function.

- **EEG (electroencephalogram)**—an amplified tracing of brain activity produced when electrodes positioned over the scalp transmit signals about the brain's electrical activity ("brain waves") to an electroencephalograph machine.

- **Evoked potentials**—EEGs resulting from a response to a specific stimulus presented to the subject.

- **Positron emission tomography (PET)**—shows brain activity when radioactively tagged glucose rushes to active neurons and emits positrons.

- **Functional MRI (fMRI)**—shows brain activity at higher resolution than the PET scan when changes in oxygen concentration near active neurons alter magnetic qualities.

Central nervous system (CNS)—brain and spinal cord.

Peripheral nervous system (PNS)—portion of the nervous system outside the brain and spinal cord; includes all of the sensory and motor neurons, and subdivisions called the autonomic and somatic nervous systems.

Autonomic nervous system (ANS)—subdivision of PNS that includes motor nerves that innervate smooth (involuntary) and heart muscle. Its sympathetic nervous system prepares the body for "fight or flight"; the parasympathetic nervous system causes bodily changes for maintenance or rest.

- **Sympathetic nervous system**—subdivision of PNS and ANS whose stimulation results in responses that help your body deal with stressful events.

- **Parasympathetic nervous system**—subdivision of PNS and ANS whose stimulation calms your body following sympathetic stimulation by restoring normal body processes.

Somatic nervous system—subdivision of PNS that includes motor nerves that stimulate skeletal (voluntary) muscles.

rod vision. Rods and cones both synapse with a second layer of neurons in front of them in your retina, called **bipolar cells.** More rods synapse with one bipolar cell than do cones. Small amounts of stimulation from each rod to a bipolar cell can enable it to fire in low light. In bright light, just one cone can stimulate a bipolar cell sufficiently to fire, providing greater visual **acuity** or resolution. Bipolar cells transmit impulses to another layer of neurons in front of them in your retina, the **ganglion cells.** Axons of these cells converge to form the **optic nerve** of each eye. Where the optic nerve exits the retina, there aren't any rods or cones, so the part of an image that falls on your retina in that area is missing—the **blind spot.** At the optic chiasm on the underside of your brain, half the axons of the optic nerve from each eye crisscross, sending impulses from the left half of each retina to the left side of your brain and from the right half of each retina to the right side of your brain. The thalamus then routes information to the primary visual cortex of your brain, where specific neurons called **feature detectors** respond only to specific features of visual stimuli, for example, a line in a particular orientation. Many different feature detectors can process the different elements of visual information, such as color, contours, orientation, and so forth, simultaneously. Simultaneous processing of stimulus elements is called **parallel processing.** David Hubel and Torsten Wiesel (1979) won a Nobel Prize for the discovery that most cells of the visual cortex respond only to particular features, such as the edge of a surface. More complex features trigger other detector cells, which respond only to complex patterns.

Color Vision

The colors of objects you see depend on the wavelengths of light reflected from those objects to your eyes. Light is the visible portion of the electromagnetic spectrum. Do you remember ROYGBIV? The letters stand for the colors red, orange, yellow, green, blue, indigo, and violet, which combine to produce white light. The colors vary in wavelength from the longest (red) to the shortest (violet). A wavelength is the distance from the top of one wave to the top of the next wave. The sun and most electric light bulbs essentially give off white light. When light hits an object, different wavelengths of light can be reflected, transmitted, or absorbed. Generally, the more lightwaves your eyes receive (the higher the amplitude of the wave), the brighter an object appears. The wavelengths of light that reach your eye from the object determine the color, or hue, the object appears to be. If an object absorbs all of the wavelengths, then none reach your eyes and the object appears black. If the object reflects all of the wavelengths, then all reach your eyes and the object appears white. If it absorbs some of the wavelengths and reflects others, the color you see results from the color(s) of the waves reflected. For example, a rose appears red when it absorbs orange, yellow, green, blue, indigo, and violet wavelengths and reflects the longer red wavelengths to your eyes.

What enables you to perceive color? In the 1800s, Thomas Young and Hermann von Helmholtz accounted for color vision with the **trichromatic theory** that three different types of photoreceptors are each most sensitive to a different range of wavelengths. People with three different types of cones are called trichromats; with two different types, dichromats; and with only one, monochromats. Cones are maximally sensitive to red, green, or blue. Each color you see results from a specific ratio of activation among the three types of receptors. For example, yellow results from stimulation of red and green cones. People who are color-blind lack a chemical usually produced by one or more types of cones. The most common type of color blindness is red–green color blindness resulting from a defective gene on the X chromosome, for a green cone chemical, or, less often, for a red cone chemical. Because it is a sex-linked recessive trait, males more frequently have this inability to distinguish colors in the red–orange–green range. Blue–yellow color blindness and total color blindness are rarer. Although trichromatic theory successfully accounts for how you can see any color in the spectrum, it cannot explain how mixing complementary colors produces

"Information about colors of light is easy to remember: COlor receptors are COnes. ROYGBIV is a long acronym, so red is a long wave. Primary colors of light and the three kinds of cones are like my computer monitor and color TV—RGB."
—Matt, AP student

the sensation of white, or why after staring at a red image, if you look at a white surface, you see green (a negative afterimage). According to Ewald Hering's **opponent-process theory,** certain neurons can be either excited or inhibited, depending on the wavelength of light, and complementary wavelengths have opposite effects. For example, the ability to see reds and greens is mediated by red–green opponent cells, which are excited by wavelengths in the red area of the spectrum and inhibited by wavelengths in the green area of the spectrum, or vice versa. The ability to see blues and yellows is similar. Black–white opponent cells determine overall brightness. This explains why mixing complementary colors red and green or blue and yellow produces the perception of white and the appearance of negative afterimages. Colors in afterimages are the complements of those in the original images. Recent physiological research essentially confirms both the trichromatic and opponent-process theories. Three different types of cones produce different photochemicals, and then cones stimulate ganglion cells in a pattern that translates the trichromatic code into an opponent-process code further processed in the thalamus.

Hearing (Audition)

In the dark, without visual stimuli that capture your attention, you can appreciate your sense of hearing, or **audition.** Evolutionarily, being able to hear approaching predators or prey in the dark, or behind one's back, helped increase chances of survival. Hearing is the primary sensory modality for human language. How do you hear? Sound waves result from the mechanical vibration of molecules from a sound source such as your vocal cords or the strings of a musical instrument. The vibrations move in a medium, such as air, outward from the source, first compressing molecules and then letting them move apart. This compression and expansion is called one cycle of a sound wave. The greater the compression, the larger the **amplitude** or height of the sound wave and the louder the sound. The amplitude is measured in logarithmic units of pressure called decibels (dB). Established by Fechner, every increase of 10 dB corresponds to a 10-fold increase in volume. The absolute threshold for hearing is 0 dB. Normal conversations measure about 60 dB. Differences in the **frequency** of the cycles, the number of complete wavelengths that pass a point in a second (hertz or Hz), determine the highness or lowness of the sound called the **pitch.** The shorter the wavelength, the higher the frequency and the higher the pitch. The longer the wavelength, the lower the frequency and the lower the pitch. People are sensitive to frequencies between about 20 and 20,000 Hz. You are best able to hear sounds with frequencies within the range that corresponds to the human voice. You can tell the difference between the notes of the same pitch and loudness played on a flute and on a violin because of a difference in the purity of the wave form or mixture of the sound waves, a difference in **timbre.**

Parts of the Ear

Your ear is well adapted for converting sound waves of vocalizations to the neural impulses you perceive as language (see Figure 7.2). Your outer ear consists of the pinna, which is the visible portion of the ear; the auditory canal, which is the opening into the head; and the eardrum or tympanum. Your outer ear channels sound waves to the eardrum that vibrates with the sound waves. This causes the three tiny bones called the ossicles (the hammer, anvil, and stirrup) of your middle ear to vibrate. The vibrating stirrup pushes against the oval window of the cochlea in the inner ear. Inside the cochlea is a basilar membrane with hair cells that are bent by the vibrations and transduce this mechanical energy to the electrochemical energy of neural impulses. Hair cells synapse with auditory neurons whose axons form the auditory nerve. The auditory nerve transmits sound messages through your medulla, pons, and thalamus to the auditory cortex of the temporal lobes. Crossing of most

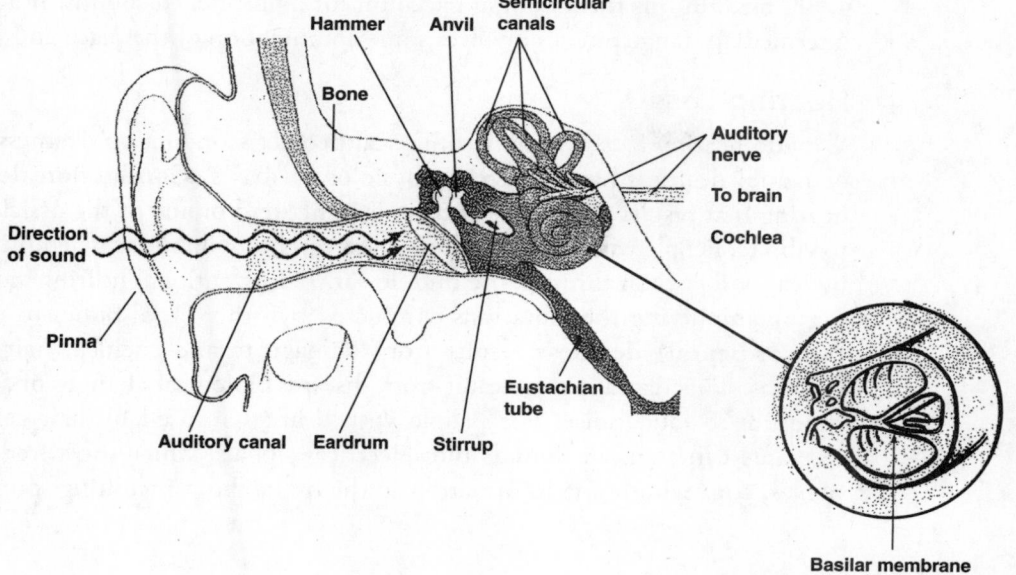

Figure 7.2   The ear.

auditory nerve fibers occurs in the medulla and pons so that your auditory cortex receives input from both ears, but contralateral input dominates.

Locating Sounds

How do you know where a sound is coming from? With ears on both sides of your head, you can locate a sound source. The process by which you determine the location of a sound is called **sound localization.** If your friend calls to you from your left side, your left ear hears a louder sound than your right ear. Using parallel processing, your brain processes both intensity differences and timing differences to determine where your friend is. The location of a sound source directly in front, behind, above, or below you is harder for you to pinpoint by hearing alone because both of your ears hear the sound simultaneously at the same intensity. You need to move your head to cause a slight offset in the sound message to your brain from each ear.

Determining Pitch

Do you know someone with perfect pitch? Many musicians can hear a melody, then play or sing it. Several theories attempt to explain how you can discriminate small differences in sound frequency or pitch. According to Georg von Békésy's **place theory,** the position on the basilar membrane at which waves reach their peak depends on the frequency of a tone. High frequencies produce waves that peak near the close end and are interpreted as high-pitched sound, while low-frequency waves travel farther, peaking at the far end, and are interpreted as low-pitched sound. Place theory accounts well for high-pitched sounds. According to **frequency theory,** the rate of the neural impulses traveling up the auditory nerve matches the frequency of a tone, enabling you to sense its pitch. Individual neurons can only fire at a maximum of 1,000 times per second. A volley mechanism in which neural cells can alternate firing can achieve a combined frequency of about 4,000 times per second. The brain can read pitch from the frequency of the neural impulses. Frequency theory, together with the volley principle, explains well how you hear low-pitched sounds of up to

4,000 Hz, but this theory doesn't account for high-pitched sounds. It appears that hearing intermediate-range pitches involves some combination of the place and frequency theories.

Hearing Loss

Why do hearing aids help only some deaf people? Conduction deafness and sensorineural or neural deafness have different physiological bases. **Conduction deafness** is a loss of hearing that results when the eardrum is punctured or any of the ossicles lose their ability to vibrate. People with conduction deafness can hear vibrations when they reach the cochlea by ways other than through the middle ear. A conventional hearing aid may restore hearing by amplifying the vibrations conducted by other facial bones to the cochlea. **Nerve (sensorineural) deafness** results from damage to the cochlea, hair cells, or auditory neurons. This damage may result from disease, biological changes of aging, or continued exposure to loud noise. For people with deafness caused by hair cell damage, cochlea implants can translate sounds into electrical signals, which are wired into the cochlea's nerves, conveying some information to the brain about incoming sounds.

Touch (Somatosensation)

Just as hearing is sensitivity to pressure on receptors in the cochlea, touch is sensitivity to pressure on the skin. Psychologists often use **somatosensation** as a general term for four classes of tactile sensations: touch/pressure, warmth, cold, and pain. Other tactile sensations result from simultaneous stimulation of more than one type of receptor. For example, burning results from stimulation of warmth, cold, and pain receptors. Itching results from repeated gentle stimulation of pain receptors, a tickle results from repeated stimulation of touch receptors, and the sensation of wetness results from simultaneous stimulation of adjacent cold and pressure receptors. Transduction of mechanical energy of pressure/touch and heat energy of warmth and cold occurs at sensory receptors distributed all over the body just below the skin's surface. Neural fibers generally carry the sensory information to your spinal cord. Information about touch usually travels quickly from your spinal cord to your medulla, where nerves crisscross, to the thalamus, arriving at the opposite sides of your somatosensory cortex in your parietal lobes. Weber used a two-point discrimination test to determine that regions such as your lips and fingertips have a greater concentration of sensory receptors than your back. The amount of cortex devoted to each area of the body is related to the sensitivity of that area. Touch is necessary for normal development and promotes a sense of well-being.

Pathways for temperature and pain are slower and less defined. You probably have a harder time localizing where you sense warmth and pain on your skin than where you sense touch or pressure. Pain is often associated with secretion of substance P, and relief from pain is often associated with secretion of endorphins. Because the experience of pain is so variable, pain requires both a biological and psychological explanation. Ronald Melzack and Patrick Wall's **gate-control theory** attempts to explain the experience of pain. You experience pain only if the pain messages can pass through a gate in the spinal cord on their route to the brain. The gate is opened by small nerve fibers that carry pain signals. Conditions that keep the gate open are anxiety, depression, and focusing on the pain. The gate is closed by neural activity of larger nerve fibers, which conduct most other sensory signals, or by information coming from the brain. Massage, electrical stimulation, acupuncture, ice, and the natural release of endorphins can influence the closing of the gate. The experience of pain alerts you to injury and often prevents further damage.

Body Senses

The body senses of kinesthesis and the vestibular sense provide information about the position of your body parts and your body movements in your environment. Close your eyes and touch your nose with your index finger. **Kinesthesis** is the system that enables you to sense the position and movement of individual parts of your body. Sensory receptors for kinesthesis are nerve endings in your muscles, tendons, and joints.

Your **vestibular sense** is your sense of equilibrium or body orientation. Your inner ear has semicircular canals at right angles to each other. Hairlike receptor cells are stimulated by acceleration caused when you turn your head. The vestibular sacs respond to straight-line accelerations with similar receptors. The combined activities of your vestibular sense, kinesthesis, and vision enable you to maintain your balance.

Chemical Senses

Gustation (taste) and **olfaction** (smell) are called chemical senses because the stimuli are molecules. Your chemical senses are important systems for warning and attraction. You won't eat rotten eggs or drink sour milk, and you can smell smoke before a sensitive household smoke detector. Evolutionarily, these adaptations increased chances of survival.

Taste receptor cells are most concentrated not only on your tongue in taste buds embedded in tissue called fungiform papillae, but are also on the roof of your mouth and the opening of your throat. Tasters have an average number of taste buds, nontasters have fewer taste buds, and supertasters have the most. You can taste only molecules that dissolve in your saliva or a liquid you drink. Scientists have identified five types of taste receptors for sweet, salty, sour, bitter, and, most recently, umami or glutamate. Babies show a preference for sweet and salty, both necessary for survival, and disgust for bitter and sour, which are characteristic of poisonous and spoiled substances. Supertasters are more sensitive than others to bitter, spicy foods and alcohol, which they find unpleasant. Each receptor is sensitive to specific chemicals that initiate an action potential. The pathway for taste messages passes to the brainstem, thalamus, and primary gustatory cortex. Receptors for different tastes activate different regions of the primary taste cortex. Our tongues also have receptors for touch, pain, cold, and warmth. The sensory interaction of taste, temperature, texture, and olfaction determine flavor.

Odor molecules reach your moist olfactory epithelium high in your nasal cavity through the nostrils of your nose and the nasal pharynx linking your nose and mouth. Dissolved odor molecules bind to receptor sites of olfactory receptors, triggering an action potential. Research has not uncovered basic odors. Axons of olfactory sensory neurons pass directly into the olfactory bulbs of the brain. Sensory information about smell is transmitted to the hypothalamus and structures in the limbic system associated with memory and emotion as well as the primary cortex for olfaction on the underside of the frontal lobes, but not the thalamus. The primary olfactory cortex is necessary for making fine distinctions among odors and using those distinctions to consciously control behavior.

Perceptual Processes

What you perceive is an active construction of reality. Perception results from the interaction of many neuron systems, each performing a simple task. Natural selection favors a perceptual system that is very efficient at picking up information needed for survival

Timbre—the quality of a sound determined by the purity of a waveform. What makes a note of the same pitch and loudness sound different on different musical instruments.

Sound localization—the process by which you determine the location of a sound.

Parts of the ear:

- The outer ear includes the pinna, the auditory canal, and the eardrum.

- The middle ear includes three tiny bones: the hammer, the anvil, and the stirrup.

- The inner ear includes the cochlea, semicircular canals, and vestibular sacs.

Cochlea—snail-shaped fluid-filled tube in the inner ear with hair cells on the basilar membrane that transduces mechanical energy of vibrating molecules to the electrochemical energy of neural impulses. Hair cell movement triggers impulses in adjacent nerve fibers.

Auditory nerve—axons of neurons in the cochlea converge transmitting sound messages through the medulla, the pons, and the thalamus to the auditory cortex of the temporal lobes.

Conduction deafness—loss of hearing that results when the eardrum is punctured or any of the ossicles lose their ability to vibrate. A hearing aid may restore hearing.

Nerve (sensorineural) deafness—loss of hearing that results from damage to the cochlea, hair cells, or auditory neurons. Cochlear implants may restore some hearing.

Place theory—the position on the basilar membrane at which waves reach their peak depends on the frequency of a tone. Accounts well for high-pitched sounds.

Frequency theory—the rate of the neural impulses traveling up the auditory nerve matches the frequency of a tone, enabling you to sense its pitch. Frequency theory explains well how you hear low-pitched sounds.

Other Senses

Somatosensation—the skin sensations: touch/pressure, warmth, cold, and pain.

Synesthesia—is a condition in which one sense (e.g., taste) is simultaneously perceived as if by one or more additional senses such as sight. Another form of synesthesia joins objects such as letters, shapes, numbers or people's names with a sensory perception such as smell, color, or flavor.

Gate-control theory—pain is experienced only if the pain messages can pass through a gate in the spinal cord on their route to the brain. The gate is opened by small nerve fibers that carry pain signals and closed by neural activity of larger nerve fibers, which conduct most other sensory signals, or by information coming from the brain.

Kinesthesis—body sense that provides information about the position and movement of individual parts of your body with receptors in muscles, tendons, and joints.

Vestibular sense—body sense of equilibrium with hairlike receptors in semicircular canals and vestibular sac in the inner ear.

Gustation—the chemical sense of taste with receptor cells in taste buds in fungiform papillae on the tongue, on the roof of the mouth, and in the throat. Molecules must dissolve to be sensed. The five basic taste sensations are sweet, sour, salty, bitter, and, newly added to the list, umami or glutamate. Flavor is the interaction of sensations of taste and odor with contributions by temperature, etc.

Olfaction—the chemical sense of smell with receptors in a mucous membrane (olfactory epithelium) on the roof of the nasal cavity. Molecules must reach the membrane and dissolve to be sensed. Olfactory receptors synapse immediately with neurons of the olfactory bulbs in the brain with no pathways to the thalamus.

Perceptual Processes

Attention—the set of processes by which you choose from among the various stimuli bombarding your senses at any instant, allowing some to be further processed by your senses and brain.

Selective attention—focused awareness of only a limited aspect of all you are capable of experiencing.

Bottom-up processing—information processing that begins with sensory receptors and works up to the brain's integration of sensory information to construct perceptions; is data-driven.

Top-down processing—information processing guided by your preexisting knowledge or expectations to construct perceptions; is concept-driven.

Perceptual constancy—perceiving an object as unchanging even when the immediate sensation of the object changes.

Visual capture—vision usually dominates when there is a conflict among senses. Gestalt psychologists recognized the importance of figure–ground in perception. They proposed organizing principles by which we perceive wholes rather than combinations of features including figure–ground, proximity, similarity, and continuity.

Depth perception—the ability to judge the distance of objects.

Monocular cues—clues about distance based on the image of one eye. Monocular cues include interposition or overlap, relative size, aerial perspective or relative clarity, texture gradient, relative height or elevation, linear perspective, relative brightness, motion parallax, and accommodation.

Binocular cues—clues about distance requiring two eyes. Binocular cues include the more important retinal disparity and less important convergence.

Optical or visual illusions—discrepancies between the appearance of a visual stimulus and its physical reality. Common examples of visual illusions include reversible figures, illusory contours, the Müller-Lyer illusion, the Ponzo illusion, and the moon illusion.

Schemas—concepts or frameworks that organize and interpret information.

CHAPTER 8

Learning

IN THIS CHAPTER

Summary: Did you have to learn how to yawn? **Learning** is a relatively permanent change in behavior as a result of experience. For a change to be considered learning, it cannot simply have resulted from maturation, inborn response tendencies, or altered states of consciousness. You didn't need to learn to yawn; you do it naturally. Learning allows you to anticipate the future from past experience and control a complex and ever-changing environment.

This chapter reviews three types of learning: classical conditioning, operant conditioning, and cognitive learning. All three emphasize the role of the environment in the learning process.

Key Ideas

- ✪ Classical conditioning
- ✪ Classical conditioning paradigm
- ✪ Classical conditioning learning curve
- ✪ Strength of conditioning
- ✪ Classical aversive conditioning
- ✪ Higher-order conditioning
- ✪ Operant conditioning
- ✪ Thorndike's instrumental conditioning
- ✪ Operant conditioning training procedures
- ✪ Operant aversive conditioning
- ✪ Reinforcers
- ✪ Operant conditioning training schedules of reinforcement
- ✪ Superstitious behavior
- ✪ Cognitive processes in learning
- ✪ The contingency model
- ✪ Latent learning
- ✪ Insight

- ✪ Social learning
- ✪ Biological factors in learning
- ✪ Preparedness evolves
- ✪ Instinctive drift

Classical Conditioning

In **classical conditioning,** the subject learns to give a response it already knows to a new stimulus. The subject associates a new stimulus with a stimulus that automatically and involuntarily brings about the response. A **stimulus** is a change in the environment that elicits (brings about) a response. A **response** is a reaction to a stimulus. When food—a stimulus—is placed in our mouths, we automatically salivate—a response. Because we do not need to learn to salivate to food, the food is an unconditional or unconditioned stimulus, and the salivation is an unconditional or unconditioned response. In the early 1900s, Russian physiologist Ivan Pavlov scientifically studied the process by which associations are established, modified, and broken. Pavlov noticed that dogs began to salivate as soon as they saw food (i.e., even before the food was placed in their mouths). The dogs were forming associations between food and events that preceded eating the food. This simple type of learning is called Pavlovian or classical conditioning.

Classical Conditioning Paradigm and the Learning Curve

In classical conditioning experiments, two stimuli, the unconditioned stimulus and neutral stimulus, are paired together. A **neutral stimulus (NS)** initially does not elicit a response. The **unconditioned stimulus (UCS** or **US)** reflexively, or automatically, brings about the **unconditioned response (UCR** or **UR).** The **conditioned stimulus (CS)** is a NS at first, but when paired with the UCS, it elicits the conditioned response (CR). During Pavlov's training trials, a bell was rung right before the meat was given to the dogs. By repeatedly pairing the food and the bell, **acquisition** of the conditioned response occurred; the bell alone came to elicit salivation in the dogs. This exemplified the classical conditioning paradigm or pattern:

reflexive behavior:	US (meat)		→	UR (salivation)
acquisition trials:	NS (bell)	+ US (meat)	→	UR (salivation)
acquisition demonstrated:	CS (bell)		→	CR (salivation)

If you are having trouble figuring out the difference between the UCS and the CS, ask yourself these questions: What did the organism LEARN to respond to? This is the CS. What did the organism respond to REFLEXIVELY? This is the US. The UCR and the CR are usually the same response.

In classical conditioning, the learner is passive and the learner *automatically/naturally* makes the association. The behaviors learned by association are elicited from the learner. The presentation of the US strengthens or reinforces the behavior. A learning curve for classical conditioning is shown in Figure 8.1.

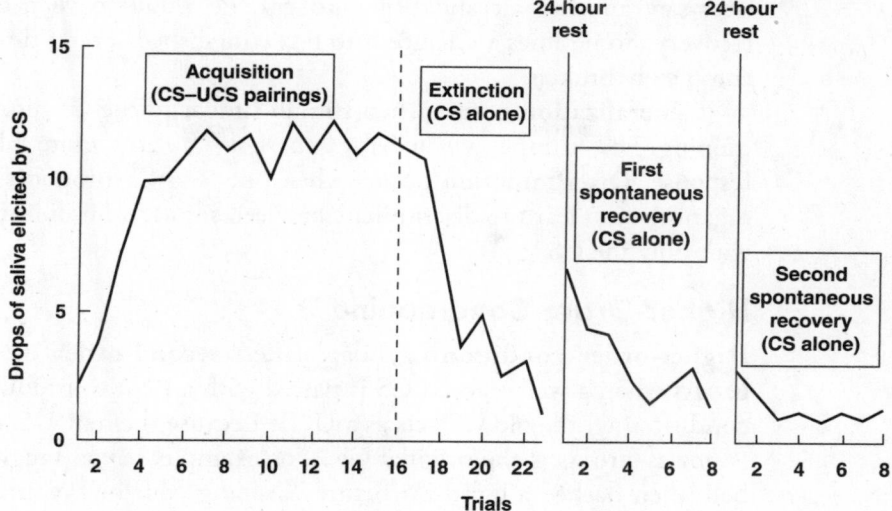

Figure 8.1   Classical conditioning learning curve.

Strength of Conditioning and Classical Aversive Conditioning

Does the timing of presentation of the NS and US matter in establishing the association for classical conditioning? Different experimental procedures have tried to determine the best presentation time for the NS and the UCS so that the NS becomes the CS.

The strength of the UCS and the saliency of the CS in determining how long acquisition takes have also been researched. In the 1920s, John B. Watson and Rosalie Rayner conditioned a 9-month-old infant known as Baby Albert to fear a rat. Their research would probably be considered unethical today. The UCS in their experiment was a loud noise made by hitting a steel rod with a hammer. Immediately Albert began to cry, a UCR. Two months later, the infant was given a harmless rat to play with. As soon as Albert went to reach for the rat (NS), the loud noise (UCS) was sounded again. Baby Albert began to cry (UCR). A week later, the rat (CS) was reintroduced to Albert, and without any additional pairings with the loud noise, Albert cried (CR) and tried to crawl away. Graphs of the learning curve in most classical conditioning experiments show a steady upward trend over many trials until the CS–UCS connection occurs. In most experiments, several trials must be conducted before acquisition occurs, but when an unconditioned stimulus is strong and the neutral stimulus is striking or salient, classical conditioning can occur in a single trial. Because the loud noise (UCS) was so strong and the white rat (CS) was salient, which means very noticeable, the connection between the two took only one trial of pairing for Albert to acquire the new CR of fear of the rat (CS). This experiment is also important because it shows how phobias and other human emotions might develop in humans through classical conditioning. Conditioning involving an unpleasant or harmful unconditioned stimulus or reinforcer, such as this conditioning of Baby Albert, is called **aversive conditioning.**

Unfortunately, Watson and Rayner did not get a chance to rid Baby Albert of his phobia of the rat. In classical conditioning, if the CS is repeatedly presented without the UCS, eventually the CS loses its ability to elicit the CR. Removal of the UCS breaks the connection and extinction, weakening of the conditioned association, occurs. If Watson had continued to present the rat (CS) and taken away the fear-inducing noise (UCS), eventually Baby Albert would probably have lost his fear of the rat. Although not fully understood by behaviorists, sometimes the extinguished response will show up again later without the re-pairing of the UCS and CS. This phenomenon is called **spontaneous recovery.** If Baby Albert had stopped crying whenever the rat appeared but 2 months

› Review Questions

Directions: For each item, choose the letter of the choice that best completes the statement or answers the question.

1. Once Pavlov's dogs learned to salivate to the sound of a tuning fork, the tuning fork was a(n)
   (A) unconditioned stimulus
   (B) neutral stimulus
   (C) conditioned stimulus
   (D) unconditioned response
   (E) conditioned response

2. Shaping is
   (A) a pattern of responses that must be made before classical conditioning is completed
   (B) rewarding behaviors that get closer and closer to the desired goal behavior
   (C) completing a set of behaviors in succession before a reward is given
   (D) giving you chocolate pudding to increase the likelihood you will eat more carrots
   (E) inhibition of new learning by previous learning

3. John loves to fish. He puts his line in the water and leaves it there until he feels a tug. On what reinforcement schedule is he rewarded?
   (A) continuous reinforcement
   (B) fixed ratio
   (C) fixed interval
   (D) variable ratio
   (E) variable interval

4. Chimpanzees given tokens for performing tricks were able to put the tokens in vending machines to get grapes. The tokens acted as
   (A) primary reinforcers
   (B) classical conditioning
   (C) secondary reinforcers
   (D) negative reinforcers
   (E) unconditioned reinforcers

5. Which of the following best reflects negative reinforcement?
   (A) Teresa is scolded when she runs through the house yelling.
   (B) Lina is not allowed to watch television until after she has finished her homework.
   (C) Greg changes his math class so he doesn't have to see his old girlfriend.
   (D) Aditya is praised for having the best essay in the class.
   (E) Alex takes the wrong medicine and gets violently ill afterward.

6. Watson and Rayner's classical conditioning of "Little Albert" was helpful in explaining that
   (A) some conditioned stimuli do not generalize
   (B) human emotions such as fear are subject to classical conditioning
   (C) drug dependency is subject to classical as well as operant conditioning
   (D) small children are not as easily conditioned as older children
   (E) fear of rats and rabbits are innate responses previously undiscovered

7. Jamel got very sick after eating some mushrooms on a pizza at his friend's house. He didn't know that he had a stomach virus at the time, blamed his illness on the mushrooms, and refused to eat them again. Which of the following is the unconditioned stimulus for his taste aversion to mushrooms?
   (A) pizza
   (B) stomach virus
   (C) mushrooms
   (D) headache
   (E) aversion to mushrooms

8. If a previous experience has given your pet the expectancy that nothing it does will prevent an aversive stimulus from occurring, it will likely
   (A) be motivated to seek comfort from you
   (B) experience learned helplessness
   (C) model the behavior of other pets in hopes of avoiding it
   (D) seek out challenges like this in the future to disprove the expectation
   (E) engage in random behaviors until one is successful in removing the stimulus

9. While readying to take a free-throw shot, you suddenly arrive at the answer to a chemistry problem you'd been working on several hours before. This is an example of
   (A) insight
   (B) backward conditioning
   (C) latent learning
   (D) discrimination
   (E) the Premack principle

10. If the trainer conditions the pigeon to peck at a red circle and then only gives him a reward if he pecks at the green circle when both a red and green circle appear, the pigeon is demonstrating
(A) matching-to-sample generalization
(B) abstract learning
(C) intrinsic motivation
(D) insight
(E) modeling

11. Latent learning is best described by which of the following?
(A) innate responses of an organism preventing new learning and associations
(B) unconscious meaning that is attributed to new response patterns
(C) response patterns that become extinguished gradually over time
(D) delayed responses that occur when new stimuli are paired with familiar ones
(E) learning that occurs in the absence of rewards

12. Rats were more likely to learn an aversion to bright lights and noise with water if they were associated with electric shocks rather than with flavors or poisoned food. This illustrates
(A) insight
(B) preparedness
(C) extinction
(D) observational learning
(E) generalization

13. Which of the following responses is NOT learned through operant conditioning?
(A) a rat learning to press a bar to get food
(B) dogs jumping over a hurdle to avoid electric shock
(C) fish swimming to the top of the tank when a light goes on
(D) pigeons learning to turn in circles for a reward
(E) studying hard for good grades on tests

14. Spontaneous recovery refers to the
(A) reacquisition of a previously learned behavior
(B) reappearance of a previously extinguished CR after a rest period
(C) return of a behavior after punishment has ended
(D) tendency of newly acquired responses to be intermittent at first
(E) organism's tendency to forget previously learned responses but to relearn them more quickly during a second training period

» Answers and Explanations

1. **C**—The tuning fork is the CS and salivation is the CR. Pavlov's dogs learned to salivate to the tuning fork.

2. **B**—The definition of shaping is reinforcing behaviors that get closer and closer to the goal.

3. **E**—Variable interval is correct. John doesn't know when a fish will be on his line. Catching fish is unrelated to the number of times he pulls in his line but rather to *when* he pulls in his line.

4. **C**—Tokens serve as secondary reinforcers the chimps learned to respond to positively. They were connected with the primary reinforcer—grapes.

5. **C**—Greg transferred from the class to avoid having to see his old girlfriend. Avoidance is one type of negative reinforcement that takes away something aversive.

6. **B**—Watson and Raynor's experiment with Little Albert showed emotional learning and phobias may be learned through classical conditioning.

7. **B**—The stomach virus is the UCS that automatically caused him to get sick. The mushrooms are the CS which he learned to avoid because of the association with the virus that caused his sickness.

8. **B**—Learned helplessness occurs when an organism has the experience that nothing it does will prevent an aversive stimulus from occurring.

9. **A**—Insight learning is the sudden appearance of a solution to a problem.

10. **B**—The animal showed understanding of a concept when it was able to tell the difference between the red and green circles and only pecked at the green circle to get a reward.

11. **E**—Latent learning is defined as learning in the absence of rewards.

12. **B**—The rats were biologically prepared to associate two external events, like shock and the lights and sounds together.

13. **C**—The fish swimming to the top of the tank when the light goes on shows classical conditioning.

14. **B**—Spontaneous recovery occurs when a conditioned response is extinguished but later reappears when the CS is present again without retraining.

» Rapid Review

Learning—a relatively permanent change in behavior as a result of experience (nurture).

Classical conditioning—learning which takes place when two or more stimuli are presented together; an unconditioned stimulus is paired repeatedly with a neutral stimulus until it acquires the capacity to elicit a similar response. The subject learns to give a response it already knows to a new stimulus. Terms and concepts associated with classical conditioning include the following:

- **Stimulus**—a change in the environment that elicits (brings about) a response.

- **Neutral stimulus (NS)**—a stimulus that initially does not elicit a response.

- **Unconditioned stimulus (UCS or US)**—reflexively, or automatically, brings about the unconditioned response.

- **Unconditioned response (UCR or UR)**—an automatic, involuntary reaction to an unconditioned stimulus.

- **Conditioned stimulus (CS)**—a neutral stimulus (NS) at first, but when paired with the UCS, it elicits the conditioned response (CR).

- **Acquisition**—in classical conditioning, learning to give a known response to a new stimulus, the neutral stimulus

US	→	UR
NS + US	→	UR
CS	→	CR

- **Extinction**—repeatedly presenting a CS without a UCS leads to return of the NS.

- **Spontaneous recovery**—after extinction and without training, the previous CS suddenly elicits the CR again temporarily.

- **Generalization**—stimuli similar to the CS also elicit the CR without training.

- **Discrimination**—the ability to tell the difference between stimuli so that only the CS elicits the CR.

- **Higher-order conditioning**—classical conditioning in which a well-learned CS is paired with an NS to produce a CR to the NS.

Aversive conditioning—learning involving an unpleasant or harmful stimulus or reinforcer.
Avoidance behavior takes away the unpleasant stimulus before it begins.
Escape behavior takes away the unpleasant stimulus after it has already started.

Instrumental learning—associative learning in which a behavior becomes more or less probable depending on its consequences.

Law of Effect—behaviors followed by positive consequences are strengthened while behaviors followed by annoying or negative consequences are weakened.

Operant conditioning—learning that occurs when an active learner performs certain voluntary behavior, and the consequences of the behavior (pleasant or unpleasant) determine the likelihood of its recurrence. Terms and concepts associated with operant conditioning include the following:

- **Positive reinforcement**—a rewarding consequence that follows a voluntary behavior thereby increasing the probability the behavior will be repeated.

- **Primary reinforcer**—something that is biologically important and, thus, rewarding.

- **Secondary reinforcer**—something rewarding because it is associated with a primary reinforcer.

- **Generalized reinforcer**—secondary reinforcer associated with a number of different primary reinforcers.

- **Premack principle**—a more probable behavior can be used as a reinforcer for a less probable one.

- **Negative reinforcement**—removal of an aversive consequence that follows a voluntary behavior, thereby increasing the probability the behavior will be repeated; two types are escape and avoidance.

- **Punishment**—an aversive consequence that follows a voluntary behavior, thereby decreasing the probability the behavior will be repeated.

- **Omission training**—removal of a rewarding consequence that follows a voluntary behavior, thereby decreasing the probability the behavior will be repeated.

words do not translate into other languages. In support of his idea, people who speak more than one language frequently report a different sense of themselves depending on the language they are speaking at the time. His **linguistic relativity hypothesis** has largely been discredited by empirical research. Rather than language determining what we can perceive, a more likely hypothesis is that the objects and events in our environment determine the words that become a part of our language.

Do you ever think about how you solve problems to attain goals? If so, you engage in **metacognition,** thinking about how you think. We usually manipulate concepts to solve problems. Concepts enable us to generalize, associate experiences and objects, access memories, and know how to react to specific experiences.

Problem Solving

How do we solve problems? Most problem-solving tasks involve a series of steps. Typically, we first identify that we have a problem. Next, we generate problem-solving strategies. These can include using an algorithm or a heuristic, or breaking the problem into smaller problems, developing *subgoals* that move us toward the solution. An **algorithm** is a problem-solving strategy that involves a slow, step-by-step procedure that guarantees a solution to many types of problems. Although we will eventually solve the problem correctly using an algorithm, we usually want to solve problems quickly and employ **heuristics** or mental shortcuts to solve most problems. For example, when we're not sure how to spell the word *receive*, rather than look up the word in the dictionary, we usually follow the heuristic "*I* before *E*, except after *C*, or when sounded like 'ay,' as in *neighbor* and *weigh*." A heuristic suggests but does not guarantee a solution to a problem and can result in incorrect solutions. Sometimes after trying to find a solution to a problem for a while, the solution suddenly comes to us. **Insight** is a sudden and often novel realization of the solution to a problem. For example, after trying to unscramble the letters NEBOTYA to form a word, you suddenly realize that the word is *bayonet*. When we don't have a clue how to solve a problem, we often start with a **trial-and-error approach.** This approach involves trying possible solutions and discarding those that do not work. If we need a combination lock for a locker and find an old lock in the drawer, we can try combinations of three numbers that come to mind, but this can be time-consuming and may not lead to a solution. Trial and error works best when choices are limited. After we have tried to solve a problem, we need to evaluate the results. How will we decide if we have solved the problem? Using critical thinking, we think reflectively and evaluate the evidence. We reason by transforming information to reach conclusions. **Inductive reasoning** involves reasoning from the specific to the general, forming concepts about all members of a category based on some members, which is often correct but may be wrong if the members we have chosen do not fairly represent all of the members. **Deductive reasoning** involves reasoning from the general to the specific. Deductions are logically correct and lead to good answers when the initial rules or assumptions are true. Have we attained our goal? Over time, we may profit from rethinking and redefining problems and solutions.

Obstacles to Problem Solving

Sometimes we are unsuccessful at solving a problem; we cannot attain our goal. What hinders our ability to solve the problem? Obstacles to problem solving and biases in reasoning can keep us from reaching a goal. **Fixation** is an inability to look at a problem from a fresh perspective, using a prior strategy that may not lead to success. If we've solved 10 problems in a 50-problem set using one rule, we tend to use the same rule to solve the 11th. This tendency to approach the problem in the same way that has been successful previously is a type of fixation called **mental set.** We may get stuck on the 11th problem because it requires a different rule from the first 10. Another type of fixation that can be an obstacle to problem solving is called **functional fixedness,** a failure to use an object in an unusual way. For example, if people are carrying plastic tablecloths to a picnic area when it starts to rain, and they get soaked because they aren't wearing raincoats and don't have umbrellas, they are evidencing functional fixedness. They could have used the tablecloths to protect them from the rain. Using decision-making heuristics when we problem solve can result in errors in our judgments. **Amos Tversky** and Nobel Prize winner **Daniel Kahneman** studied how and why people make illogical choices. They looked at two types of research. Normative studies ask how we *ought* to make decisions and do not actually reflect how people make decisions. Descriptive studies look at how decisions are actually being made. Tversky and Kahneman found we often make erroneous decisions based on intuition. Under conditions of uncertainty, we often use the **availability heuristic,** estimating the probability of certain events in terms of how readily they come to mind. For example, many people who think nothing of taking a ride in a car are afraid to ride in an airplane because they think it is so dangerous. In fact, riding in an airplane is much safer; we are far less likely to be injured or die as a result of riding in an airplane. Other errors in decision making result from using the **representative heuristic,** a mental shortcut by which a new situation is judged by how well it matches a stereotypical model or a particular prototype. Is someone who loves to solve math problems more likely to be a mathematics professor or a high school student? Although many people immediately reply that it must be the professor, the correct answer to the problem is the high school student. The total number of high school students is so much greater than the total number of mathematics professors that even if only a small fraction of high school students love to solve math problems, there will be many more of them than mathematics professors. **Framing** refers to the way a problem is posed. How an issue is framed can significantly affect people's perceptions, decisions, and judgments. We are more likely to buy a product that says it is 90 percent fat-free, than if it says it contains 10 percent fat. A suggestion can have a powerful effect on how we respond to a problem. Kahneman and Tversky asked if the length of the Mississippi River is longer or shorter than some suggested length and then asked how long the person thinks the river actually is. When the suggested length was 500 miles, the length guessed was much smaller than when the suggested length was 5,000 miles. The **anchoring effect** is this tendency to be influenced by a suggested reference point, pulling our response toward that point.

Biases

Confirmation bias is a tendency to search for and use information that supports our preconceptions and ignore information that refutes our ideas. To lessen this tendency, we can consider the opposite. **Belief perseverance** is a tendency to hold onto a belief after the basis for the belief is discredited. This is different from **belief bias,** the tendency for our preexisting beliefs to distort logical reasoning, making illogical conclusions seem valid or logical conclusions seem invalid. **Hindsight bias** is a tendency to falsely report, after the event, that we correctly predicted the outcome of the event. Finally, the **overconfidence bias** is a tendency to underestimate the extent to which our judgments are erroneous. For example, when reading this section dealing with obstacles to problem solving and errors in decision making, we tend to think that we make these errors less often than most other people do.

Creativity

Creativity is the ability to think about a problem or idea in new and unusual ways, to come up with unconventional solutions. One way to overcome obstacles to problem solving and avoid biases in reasoning is to borrow strategies from creative problem solvers.

Convergent thinkers use problem-solving strategies directed toward one correct solution to a problem, whereas **divergent thinkers** produce many answers to the same question, characteristic of creativity. When they feel stuck on a particular problem, creative thinkers tend to move on to others. Later they come back to those stumpers with a fresh approach. To combat the confirmation and overconfidence biases, when beginning to solve a problem, creative problem solvers **brainstorm,** generating lots of ideas without evaluating them. After collecting as many ideas as possible, solutions are reviewed and evaluated.

Standardization and Norms

Psychometrics is the measurement of mental traits, abilities, and processes. **Psychometricians** are involved in test development in order to measure some *construct* or behavior that distinguishes people. Constructs are ideas that help summarize a group of related phenomena or objects; they are hypothetical abstractions related to behavior and defined by groups of objects or events. For example, we can't measure happiness, honesty, or intelligence in feet or meters. If someone tells the truth in a wide variety of situations, however, we might consider that person honest. Although we cannot observe happiness, honesty, or intelligence directly, they are useful concepts for understanding, describing, and predicting behavior. Psychological tests include tests of abilities, interests, creativity, personality, and intelligence. A good test is standardized, reliable, and valid. After many questions for a test have been written, edited, and pretested, questions are thrown out if nearly everyone answers them correctly or if very few answer them right because these types of questions do not tell us anything about individual differences. Tests that differentiate among test takers and that are composed of questions that fairly test all aspects of the behavior to be assessed are assembled. They are then administered to a sample of hundreds or thousands of people who fairly represent all of the people who are likely to take the test. This sample is used to standardize the test. **Standardization** is a two-part test development procedure that first establishes test norms from the test results of the large representative sample that initially took the test and then ensures that the test is both administered and scored uniformly for all test takers. **Norms** are scores established from the test results of the representative sample, which are then used as a standard for assessing the performances of subsequent test takers; more simply, norms are standards used to compare scores of test takers. For example, the mean score for the SAT is 500 and the standard deviation is 100, whereas the mean score for the Wechsler Adult Intelligence Scale (IQ test) is 100 and the standard deviation is 15, based on the "standardization" sample. When administering a standardized test, all proctors must give the same directions and time limits and provide the same conditions as all other proctors. All scorers must use the same scoring system, applying the same standards to rate responses as all other scorers. Thus, we should earn the same test score no matter where we take the test or who scores it.

Reliability and Validity

Not only must a good test be standardized, but it must also be reliable and valid.

Reliability

If a test is reliable, we should obtain the same score no matter where, when, or how many times we take it (if other variables remain the same). Several methods are used to determine if a test is reliable. In the *test-retest* method, the same exam is administered to the same group on two different occasions, and the scores compared. The closer the correlation coefficient is to 1.0, the more reliable the test. The problem with this method of determining reliability or consistency is that performance on the second test may be better because test takers are already familiar with the questions and test procedures. In the *split-half* method, the score on one half of the test questions is correlated with the score on the other half of the questions to see if they are consistent. One way to do that might be to compare the score of all the odd-numbered questions to the score of all the even-numbered questions. In the *alternate form method* or *equivalent form method,* two different versions of a test on the same material are given to the same test takers, and the scores are correlated. The SAT given on Saturday is different from the SAT given on Sunday in October; there are different questions on each form. Although this does not happen, if the same people took both exams and the tests were highly reliable, the scores should be the same on both tests. This would also necessitate high *interrater reliability,* the extent to which two or more scorers evaluate the responses in the same way.

Validity

Tests can be very reliable, but if they are not also valid, they are useless for measuring the particular construct or behavior. Psychometricians must present data to show that a test measures what it is supposed to measure accurately and that the results can be used to make accurate decisions. Because there are no universal standards against which test scores can be compared, validation is most frequently accomplished by obtaining high correlations between the test and other assessments. **Validity** is the extent to which an instrument accurately measures or predicts what it is supposed to measure or predict. Just as there are several methods for measuring reliability, there are also several methods for measuring validity.

Types of Tests

Ask different psychometricians to categorize types of tests, and they may give different answers, because tests can be categorized along many dimensions.

Performance, Observational, and Self-Report Tests

Psychological tests can be sorted into the three categories of performance tests, observational tests, and self-report tests. For a performance test, the test taker knows what he or she should do in response to questions or tasks on the test, and it is assumed that the test taker will do the best he or she can to succeed. Performance tests include the SATs, AP tests, **Wechsler intelligence tests, Stanford–Binet intelligence tests,** and most classroom tests, including finals, as well as computer tests and road tests for a driver's license. Observational tests differ from performance tests in that the person being tested does not have a single, well-defined task to perform but rather is assessed on typical behavior or performance in a specific context. Employment interviews and formal on-the-job observations for evaluation by supervisors are examples of observational tests. Self-report tests require the test taker to describe his or her feelings, attitudes, beliefs, values, opinions, physical state, or mental state on surveys, questionnaires, or polls. The **MMPI-2** (described in Chapter 14) exemplifies the self-report test.

Performance tests in which there is a correct answer for each item can be divided into two types: *speed tests* and *power tests. Speed tests* generally include a large number of relatively easy items administered with strict time limits under which most test takers find it impossible to answer all questions. Given more time, many test takers would probably score higher, so differences in scores among test takers are at least partly a function of the speed with

› Rapid Review

Memory—human capacity to register, retain, and remember information.

Three models of memory:

1. **Information processing model** of memory—encoding, storage, and retrieval.

   - **Encoding**—the process of putting information into the memory system.

   - **Storage**—the retention of encoded information over time.

   - **Retrieval**—the process of getting information out of memory storage.

   We have difficulty attending to two complex tasks—divided attention.

2. **Levels of processing theory** or **semantic network theory**—the ability to form memories depends upon the depth of the processing.

   - **Shallow processing**—structural encoding emphasizes structure of incoming sensory information.

   - **Deep processing**—semantic encoding involves forming an association or attaching meaning to a sensory impression and results in longer-lasting memories.

   Self-reference effect or **self-referent encoding**—processing information deemed important or relevant more deeply, making it easier to recall.

3. Atkinson–Shiffrin model: Three memory systems—sensory, short term, and long term.

   - **Sensory memory**—memory system that holds external events from the senses for up to a few seconds.

     - **Visual encoding**—the encoding of picture images.

     - **Iconic memory**—a momentary sensory memory of visual stimuli.

     - **Acoustic encoding**—the encoding of sound, especially the sound of words.

     - **Echoic memory**—a momentary sensory memory of auditory stimuli.

     - **Selective attention**—the focusing of awareness on stimuli in sensory memory that facilitates its encoding into STM.

     - **Automatic processing**—unconscious encoding of information about space, time, and frequency that occurs without interfering with our thinking about other things.

     - **Parallel processing**—a natural mode of information processing that involves several information streams simultaneously.

     - **Effortful processing**—encoding that requires our attention and conscious effort.

     - **Feature extraction (pattern recognition)**—finding a match for new raw information in sensory storage by actively searching through long-term memory.

   - **Short-term memory (STM)**—working memory, 20 seconds before forgotten; capacity of seven plus or minus two items.

     - **Rehearsal**—conscious repetition of information to either maintain information in STM or to encode it for storage.

- **Maintenance rehearsal**—repetition that keeps information in STM about 20 seconds.

- **Elaborative rehearsal**—repetition that creates associations between the new memory and existing memories stored in LTM.

- **Chunking**—grouping information into meaningful units increasing the capacity of STM.

- **Mnemonic devices**—memory tricks or strategies to make information easier to remember.

- **Method of loci**—uses visualization with familiar objects on a path to recall information in a list.

- **Peg word system**—uses association of terms to be remembered with a memorized scheme ("One is a bun, two is . . .").

- **Long-term memory (LTM)**—relatively permanent storage with unlimited capacity, LTM is subdivided into explicit (declarative) memory and implicit memory.

  - **Explicit memory (declarative)**—memory of facts and experiences that one consciously knows and can verbalize. Explicit memory is subdivided into **semantic memory** (memory of general knowledge or objective facts) and **episodic memory** (memory of personally experienced events).

  - **Implicit memory (nondeclarative)**—retention without conscious recollection of learning the skills and dispositions. Implicit memory includes **procedural memory**—memories of perceptual, motor, and cognitive skills.

Four major models account for organization of information in LTM:

1. **Hierarchies**—systems in which concepts are arranged from more general to more specific classes.

   Concepts—mental representations of related things.

   Prototypes—the most typical examples of a concept.

2. **Semantic networks**—more irregular and distorted systems than strict hierarchies, with multiple links from one concept to others.

3. **Schemas**—frameworks of basic ideas and preconceptions about people, objects, and events based on past experience.

   Script—a schema for an event.

4. **Connectionism**—theory that memory is stored throughout the brain in connections between neurons, many of which can work together to process a single memory.

Artificial intelligence (AI)—a field of study in which computer programs are designed to simulate human cognitive abilities such as reasoning, learning, and understanding language.

Neural network or parallel processing model—clusters of neurons that are interconnected (and computer models based on neuronlike systems) and process information simultaneously, automatically, and without our awareness.

Long-term potentiation or LTP—an increase in a synapse's firing potential after brief, rapid stimulation and possibly the neural basis for learning and memory, involving an increase in the efficiency with which signals are sent across the synapses within neural networks.

The biology of memory:

- The **thalamus** is involved in encoding sensory memory into STM.

- The **hippocampus** is involved in putting information from STM into LTM.

- The **amygdala** is involved in the storage of emotional memories.

- The **cerebellum** processes implicit memories and seems to store procedural memory and classically conditioned memories.

- The **basal ganglia** process implicit memories.

Retrieval—the process of getting information out of memory storage. Key terms and concepts associated with retrieval include the following:

- **Retrieval cue**—a stimulus that provides a trigger to get an item out of memory.

- **Priming**—activating specific associations in memory either consciously or unconsciously.

- **Recognition**—identification of something as familiar such as multiple-choice and matching questions on a test.

- **Recall**—retrieval of information from LTM in the absence of any other information or cues such as for an essay question or fill-in question on a test.

- **Reconstruction**—retrieval that can be distorted by adding, dropping, or changing details to complete a picture from incomplete stored information.

- **Confabulation**—process of combining and substituting memories from events other than the one you're trying to remember.

- **Flashbulb memory**—vivid memory of an emotionally significant moment or event.

- **Misinformation effect**—incorporation of misleading information into memories of a given event.

- **Serial position effect**—better recall for information that comes at the beginning **(primacy effect)** and at the end of a list of words **(recency effect)**.

- **Encoding specificity principle**—retrieval depends upon the match between the way information is encoded and the way it is retrieved.

- **Context-dependent memory**—physical setting in which a person learns information is encoded along with the information and becomes part of the memory trace.

- **Mood congruence (mood-dependent memory)**—tendency to recall experiences that are consistent with one's current good or bad mood.

- **State-dependent memory effect**—tendency to recall information better when in the same internal state as when the information was encoded.

- **Distributed practice**—spreading out the memorization of information or the learning of skills over several sessions typically produces better retrieval than massed practice.

- **Massed practice**—cramming the memorization of information or the learning of skills into one session.

Forgetting—the inability to retrieve information. Forgetting results from failure to encode, decay of stored memories, or inability to access stored information. Key terms and concepts associated with memory include the following:

- **Interference**—learning some items prevents retrieving others, especially when the items are similar.

- **Proactive interference**—the process by which old memories prevent the retrieval of newer memories.

- **Retroactive inference**—the process by which new memories prevent the retrieval of older memories.

- **Repression**—the tendency to forget unpleasant or traumatic memories hidden in the unconscious mind, according to Freud.

- **Tip-of-the-tongue phenomenon**—the often temporary inability to access information accompanied by a feeling that the information is in LTM.

- **Anterograde amnesia**—inability to put new information into explicit memory resulting from damage to hippocampus; no new semantic memories are formed.

- **Retrograde amnesia**—memory loss for a segment of the past, usually around the time of an accident.

Overlearning—continuing to practice after memorizing information makes it more resistant to forgetting.

Cognition—all the mental activities associated with thinking, knowing, and remembering.

Metacognition—thinking about how you think.

Problem-solving steps typically involve identifying a problem, generating problem-solving strategies, trying a strategy, and evaluating the results.

Trial and error—trying possible solutions and discarding those that fail to solve the problem.

Algorithm—problem-solving strategy that involves a step-by-step procedure that guarantees a solution to certain types of problems.

Heuristic—a problem-solving strategy used as a mental shortcut to quickly simplify and solve a problem, but that does not guarantee a correct solution.

Insight learning—the sudden appearance (often creative) or awareness of a solution to a problem.

Deductive reasoning—reasoning from the general to the specific.

Inductive reasoning—reasoning from the specific to the general.

Hindrances to problem solving may include the following:

- **Mental sets**—barriers to problem solving that occur when we apply only methods that have worked in the past rather than trying new or different strategies.

- **Functional fixedness**—when we are not able to recognize novel uses for an object because we are so familiar with its common use.

- **Cognitive illusion**—systematic way of thinking that is responsible for an error in judgment.

or rapid learning—generally diminishes with aging, **crystallized intelligence**—learned knowledge and skills such as vocabulary—generally improves with age (at least through the 60s). In situations that access their skills and long-term memories, older adults may show superior functioning to younger people but with tasks that require effort, initiative, and speed may show decline. Decline in mental abilities can be slowed if we stay healthy, live in a favorable environment, engage in stimulating activities, are flexible, have a mentally able partner, maintain perceptual processing speed, and feel satisfied with our earlier accomplishments.

Theories of Moral Development

Moral development refers to growth in the ability to tell right from wrong, control impulses, and act ethically. **Lawrence Kohlberg**, like Piaget, thought that moral thinking develops sequentially in stages as cognitive abilities develop. Kohlberg examined moral development by asking boys, male adolescents, and men how they would solve hypothetical moral problems, the most famous one dealing with Heinz, who must decide whether or not to steal a scarce drug he is unable to pay for in order to possibly save his wife's life. Kohlberg analyzed the reasoning subjects used to arrive at their answers. Kohlberg concluded that our moral reasoning develops from simple and concrete to more abstract and principled. He suggested three basic levels of moral development consisting of two stages each:

- When at the preoperational stage of cognitive development, children tend to be at the **preconventional** level of morality, in which they do the right thing to avoid punishment (stage 1) or to further their self-interests (stage 2).
- When at the concrete operational stage of cognitive development, people tend to move on to the **conventional** level of morality, in which they follow rules to live up to the expectations of others, "good boy/nice girl" (stage 3), or to maintain "law and order" and do their duty (stage 4). Most teenagers and adults think morally at the conventional level.
- Some people who are in the formal operational stage of cognitive development progress to Kohlberg's third or **postconventional** level of morality, in which they evidence a social contract orientation that promotes the society's welfare (stage 5) or evidence an ethical principle orientation that promotes justice and avoids self-condemnation (stage 6).

Studies by other researchers show the same sequence of stages in moral development for stages 1 through 4. According to cross-cultural studies, people in individualistic societies, such as North Americans and Europeans, are more likely to show Kohlberg's postconventional morality than those in collectivistic societies who value community standards over personal standards.

Applying Kohlberg's scale to women, **Carol Gilligan** found that women rarely reach the highest stages of morality, because they think more about the caring thing to do or following an ethic of care, rather than what the rules allow or following an ethic of justice. She asserted that women are not morally inferior, just different. Subsequent studies by other researchers have found that both men and women use both justice and care dimensions in their moral reasoning. Other critics point out that people are often inconsistent in their moral reasoning, even when dealing with their own moral dilemmas. They also suggest that since both cultural factors and cognitive factors influence moral development, moral ideals are not universal.

Theories of Social and Emotional Development

Theories of **social development** look at the influence of others on the development of a person. Others include members of the family and other caregivers, peers, and even **culture,** which consists of the behaviors, ideas, attitudes, and traditions transmitted from one generation to the next within a group of people who share the same language and environment.

Interactions Between Babies and Parents

Interactions aren't objective; they involve emotions. *Bonding* is the creation of a close emotional relationship between the mother (or parents) and baby shortly after birth.

Attachment

As the mother (or other caregiver) bonds with the infant, through frequent interactions, the infant gradually forms a close emotional relationship with his or her mother (or other caregivers), a process called **attachment.** A half century ago, developmental psychologists thought that babies became attached to the caregiver who fed them. **Harry Harlow**'s experimental research with monkeys disproved that belief when he found that baby monkeys separated from their mothers preferred to spend time with and sought comfort from a soft cloth-covered substitute (surrogate) rather than a bare wire substitute with a feeding bottle. More recent research has revealed that human infants become attached to familiar caregivers, usually parents, who not only provide them with nourishment but also a soft, warm, reassuring environment where the baby feels safe and secure.

Secure and Insecure Attachment

Mary Ainsworth studied attachment using a "strange situation" where a mother and baby play in an unfamiliar room, the baby interacts with the mother and an unfamiliar woman, the mother leaves the baby with the other woman briefly, the baby is left alone briefly, and then the mother returns to the room. A majority of babies played happily when their mothers were present, explored their environment, and returned to their mothers periodically, and when their mothers returned after an absence, they were happy to see them and receptive to their contact, displaying *secure attachment.* The mothers were generally sensitive and responsive to their babies' needs. On the other hand, some babies showed *insecure attachment.* When their mothers were present, they avoided or ignored them and were upset when they left but were angry and rejected them when they returned, or they behaved inconsistently. Securely attached babies tend to become socially competent children.

Temperament

The baby's **temperament,** or natural disposition to show a particular mood at a particular intensity for a specific period, affects his or her behavior. Both the infant's heredity and his or her intrauterine environment affect whether the neonate is easy or difficult. *Easy* babies are cheerful, relaxed, and follow predictable patterns of eating and sleeping, while *difficult* babies are irritable, intense, and unpredictable. In general, easy babies tend to become sociable children, and difficult babies tend to become less sociable children. How the primary caregiver responds to the baby affects how the baby will react to an extent. Jerome Kagan showed that shy, inhibited babies can become more relaxed and less fearful with responsive parenting.

Awareness of Self and Others

Becoming aware of ourselves and others is crucial to social development. **Self-awareness,** consciousness of oneself as a person, and **social referencing,** observing the behavior of others in social situations to obtain information or guidance, both develop between ages 1 and 2. The "rouge test," in which a red spot is secretly put on a baby's nose, then the baby is placed in front of a mirror to see if the baby realizes it is his or her own nose with the red spot, has revealed that self-awareness typically develops at age $1\frac{1}{2}$.

Parenting Styles

Diana Baumrind studied how parenting styles affect the emotional growth of children. **Authoritarian** parents set up strict rules, expect children to follow them, and punish wrongdoing. In contrast, more democratic **authoritative** parents set limits but explain the reasons for rules with their children and make exceptions when appropriate. **Permissive** parents tend not to set firm guidelines, if they set any at all. They tend to be more responsive than demanding. **Uninvolved** parents make few demands, show low responsiveness, and communicate little with their children. While these parents fulfill the children's basic needs, they are generally detached from their children's lives. In extreme cases, these parents may even reject or neglect the needs of their children. Baumrind and other researchers found that for European and American families, the most self-reliant, socially competent children with the highest self-esteem have warm, authoritative parents. Since these findings come from correlational studies, they do not establish cause and effect.

Erikson's Stage Theory of Psychosocial Development

Parents are not the only people who interact with children; each stage of development requires a new level of social interaction. Starting with kindergarten, frequent peer interactions become more complex and structured and lead to friendships. Peer interactions help children develop social skills such as cooperation, empathy, and self-regulation. **Erik Erikson** was an influential theorist partly because he examined development across the life span in a social context, rather than just during childhood, recognizing that we continue to grow beyond our teenage years, and our growth is influenced by others. His stage theory of *psychosocial development* identifies eight stages during which we face an important issue or crisis. How we resolve each crisis shapes our personality and affects our relationships with others see the Table 10.2.

Table 10.2 Erik Erikson's Theory of Psychosocial Development

Stage	Period	Crisis	Positive Resolution
1	First year	Trust vs. mistrust	Sense of security
2	Second year	Autonomy vs. shame/doubt	Sense of independence
3	3–5 years	Initiative vs. guilt	Balance between spontaneity and restraint
4	6 years to puberty	Industry vs. inferiority	Sense of self-confidence
5	Adolescence	Identity vs. role confusion	Unified sense of self
6	Young adulthood	Intimacy vs. isolation	Form close personal relationships
7	Middle adulthood	Generativity vs. stagnation	Promote well-being of others
8	Late adulthood	Integrity vs. despair	Sense of satisfaction with life well lived

> "So that you don't get authoritarian and authoritative parenting mixed up, remember authoritarian is like totalitarian (that we learned about in social studies). Both authoritarians and totalitarians exercise complete control and authority over people's lives."
> —Shereen, AP student

- **Stage One:** Infants (newborn to 1 year old) face the crisis of *trust vs. mistrust.* Parents must provide a safe, consistent, and loving environment for children to leave this stage healthily with a strong trust that others care and will always be there for them. Mistrust, based on inconsistent, cold, or abusive situations, prevents children from leaving this stage ready to form lasting and close relationships in the future.
- **Stage Two:** Toddlers (2 years old) face the crisis of *autonomy vs. shame and doubt.* The nickname "terrible twos" comes from children's needs to develop self-control and do things for themselves, which can often result in spills, falls, wetting, and other accidents. Children who are encouraged to try new skills develop autonomy, while those who are ridiculed or overprotected may doubt their abilities and feel ashamed of their actions.
- **Stage Three:** Children (3–5 years of age) face the crisis of *initiative vs. guilt.* Children need to learn to make plans and carry out tasks through play, asking questions, making choices, and using their imaginations to develop initiative. If they are severely criticized, discouraged from asking questions, not permitted to make choices, or prevented from playing, children feel guilty.
- **Stage Four:** School-aged children (6–12 years of age) face the crisis of *industry vs. inferiority.* Children need to be positively reinforced for productive activities, such as achieving in the classroom, on the sports field, or artistically or musically, in order to develop a healthy self-concept and a sense of industry. If children's efforts are considered inadequate, feelings of social or mental inferiority in this stage can carry over to a poor self-concept in the future.
- **Stage Five:** The crisis of stage five for adolescents (about 12–20 years of age) is *identity vs. role confusion.* Answering the question, "Who am I?" is the major task, which involves building a consistent identity, a unified sense of self. During adolescence, peer relationships become much more important. Because family and peer groups often have different values, attitudes, beliefs, and perspectives, adolescents are faced with opportunities and challenges to define themselves. Failure of teens to achieve a sense of identity results in role confusion and uncertainty about who they are and where they are going.
- **Stage Six:** Young adults (about 21–40 years of age) face the crisis of *intimacy vs. isolation.* Intimacy involves deeply caring about others and sharing meaningful experiences with them, especially a life partner. Without intimacy, people feel alone and uncared for in life; they experience isolation.
- **Stage Seven:** In middle adulthood (about 40–65 years of age), the crisis is *generativity vs. stagnation.* During this period, adults need to express their caring about the next and future generations by guiding or mentoring others or producing creative work that enriches the lives of others. People who fail to achieve generativity can become stagnant and preoccupied with their own needs and comforts.
- **Stage Eight:** In late adulthood (about age 65 to death), the crisis is *integrity vs. despair.* Those who look back on their lives with satisfaction that they have lived their lives well develop a sense of wholeness and integrity. Those in despair look back with regrets and disappointment in the lives they've led.

Erikson's theory most accurately describes development in individualistic societies.

Middle Age and Death

Daniel Levinson described a midlife transition period at about age 40, seen by some as a last chance to achieve their goals. People who experience anxiety, instability, and change about themselves, their work, and their relationships during this time have a challenging experience sometimes termed *the mid-life crisis.*

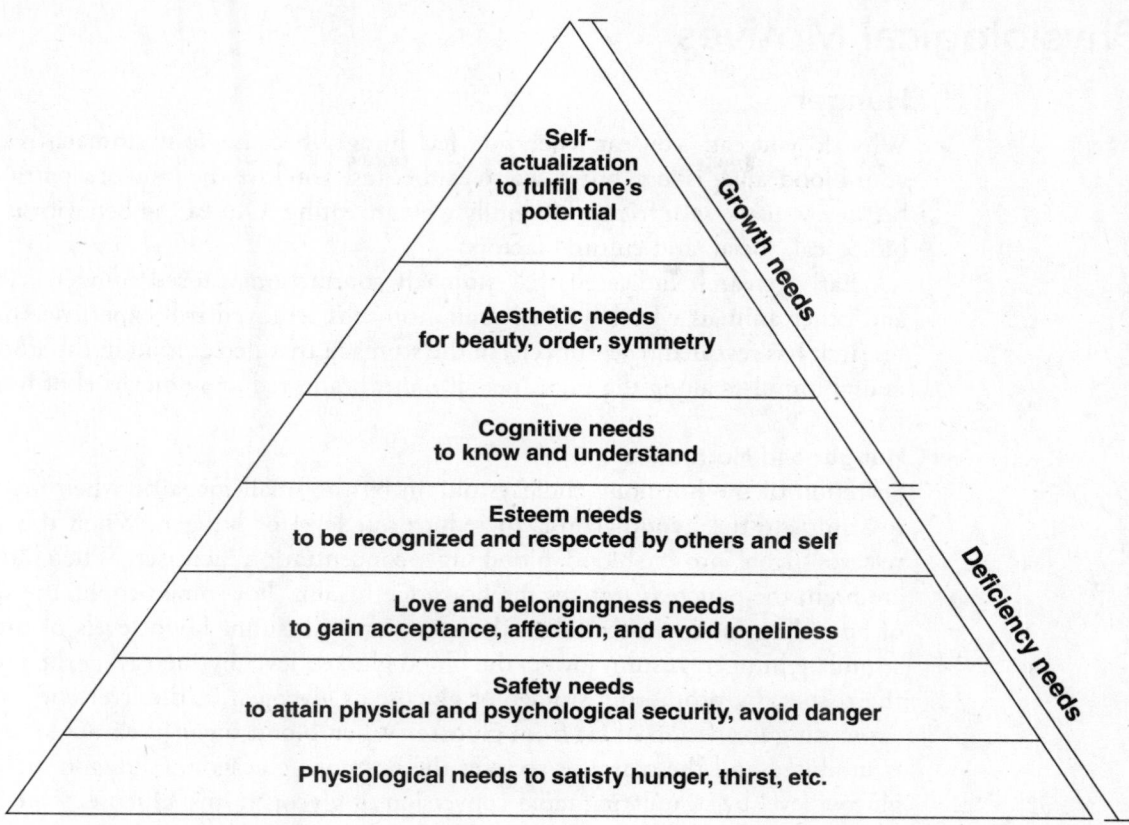

Figure 11.1 Maslow's hierarchy of needs.

we tend to perform very easy or well-learned tasks at a higher level of arousal. When first learning to drive a car, we will drive best if we are not anxious about our performance. Years later, we may need the radio on while we are driving to keep us aroused for our best performance.

Maslow's Hierarchy of Needs

Humanistic psychologist Abraham Maslow categorized needs and then arranged them in order of priority, starting with powerful physiological needs, such as the needs for food and water. His hierarchy is often pictured as a pyramid (Figure 11.1). Maslow agreed with Hull that basic biological needs to satisfy hunger and thirst must be met first, followed by our safety needs to feel safe, secure, and stable in a world that is organized and predictable. When our stomachs are growling because we are hungry and homeless, it is unlikely that our greatest motivation will be to get a high grade on a test. When our needs for food, drink, shelter, and safety have been met, we are motivated to meet our belongingness and love needs, to love and be loved, to be accepted by others and considered part of a group, such as a family, and to avoid loneliness and alienation. This need is followed by esteem needs for self-esteem, achievement, competence, and independence and the need for recognition and respect from others. According to Maslow, few people reach the highest levels of **self-actualization,** which is achievement of all of our potentials, and *transcendence,* which is spiritual fulfillment. Although this theory is attractive, we do not always place our highest priority on meeting lower-level needs. Political activists go on hunger strikes, soldiers sacrifice their lives, and parents go without food in order to feed their children. Scientific evidence does not support this theory.

Physiological Motives

Hunger

Why do you eat? You eat when you feel hungry because your stomach is contracting or your blood sugar is low, but you also eat because you love the taste of a particular food, and because you are with friends or family who are eating. Our eating behavior is influenced by biological, social, and cultural factors.

Early research indicated that stomach contractions caused hunger. Yet even people and other animals who have had their stomachs removed still experience hunger. Recent research has revealed receptor cells in the stomach that detect food in the stomach and send neural impulses along the vagus nerve to our brain, reducing our level of hunger.

Hunger and Hormones

Secretion of the hormone cholecystokinin by the small intestine when food enters seems to stimulate the hypothalamus to reduce our level of hunger. When the small intestine releases sugars into the blood, blood sugar concentration increases. When blood sugar levels are high, the pancreas secretes the hormone insulin. For some people, the sight and smell of appealing food can stimulate the secretion of insulin. High levels of insulin generally stimulate hunger. Insulin lowers the blood glucose level by increasing the use of glucose in the tissues, by promoting storage of glucose as glycogen in the liver and muscles, and by promoting formation of fat from glucose. When blood sugar levels are low, insulin release is inhibited and the pancreas secretes the hormone glucagon. Glucagon increases the blood glucose level by stimulating rapid conversion of glycogen into glucose, which is released by the liver and muscles into the bloodstream. Thus, insulin and glucagon work antagonistically through a negative feedback loop to help maintain homeostasis. Other secretions seem involved in hunger also, such as ghrelin secreted by an empty stomach that signals hunger and leptin secreted by fat cells that decreases hunger.

Hunger and the Hypothalmus

Neurons in the liver sensitive to glucose in the surrounding fluid send signals to the hypothalamus by way of the vagus nerve. Three parts of the hypothalamus in the brain seem to integrate information about hunger and satisfaction or satiety. The **lateral hypothalamus (LH)** was originally called the "on" button for hunger. When stimulated, this structure of the brain will start eating behavior, but if it is lesioned or removed, the individual will not eat at all and will even starve to death. The **ventromedial hypothalamus (VMH)** was called the satiety center, or "off" button, for hunger. When stimulated, it turns off the urge to eat and when removed, the organism will continue to eat excessively and gain weight rapidly. Recent research indicates that a third region of the hypothalamus called the paraventricular nucleus (PVN) also helps regulate eating behavior as a result of stimulation or inhibition by neurotransmitters. Norepinephrine, GABA, and neuropeptide Y seem to increase the desire for carbohydrates, whereas serotonin seems to decrease the desire for carbohydrates. When the hormone leptin, produced by fat cells, is released into the bloodstream, it acts on receptors in the brain to inhibit release of neuropeptide Y into the PVN, thus inhibiting eating behavior.

Eating and Environmental Factors

Although eating behavior is partially regulated by biological factors, environmental factors such as learned preferences, food-related cues, and stress also influence our desire to eat. We all seem to have some inborn taste preferences for sweet foods, salty foods, and high-fat foods, but learning also influences what we eat. People from different cultures show different patterns of food consumption. Meat and potatoes are consumed in larger quantities in the United States, while rice and fish are the staple foods in Japan. Religious values also influence eating behavior by setting specific rules for the foods we may eat and those we are not permitted to eat. Finally, we tend to learn our food habits from our parents, partly by observational learning and partly by classical conditioning, for example, by pairing foods with pleasant social interactions. What, how often, and how much we should eat are expectations we have learned since we were babies.

Obesity

Obesity and the potential for health problems associated with diabetes and hypertension are growing concerns in our population. People of normal weight tend to respond to internal, long-term bodily cues, such as stomach contractions and glucose–insulin levels, while those who are obese tend to pay more attention to the short-term, external cues, such as smell, attractiveness of food, and whether it is mealtime. Stress-induced arousal also stimulates eating behavior in a large proportion of the population.

Aware that obesity often leads to health problems and that millions of people try to lose weight, scientists have studied obesity and weight loss. By studying identical twins who were raised apart, they have found that some people inherit a predisposition to be overweight, while others have a predisposition to be too thin. Most people who lose weight on diets tend to put it back on. Most people who try to gain weight have difficulty keeping their weight up. These observations led to the set-point theory, that we each have a **set point,** or a preset natural body weight, determined by the number of fat cells in our body. When we eat less, our weight goes down and our fat cells contract, which seems to trigger processes that result in decreased metabolism and increased hunger. When we eat more, our weight goes up and our fat cells increase in size, which seems to result in increased metabolism and decreased hunger. If we continue to eat more, we can continue to gain weight, and our set point can go up. Some scientists theorize that many chronic dieters are restrained eaters who stringently control their eating impulses and feel guilty when they fail. They become disinhibited and eat excessively if their control is disrupted, which contributes to weight gain.

Eating Disorders

Slim models and actresses in the media are pictured as ideals in America and in some European countries. Some people are highly motivated to achieve this ideal weight, and develop eating disorders. Underweight people who weigh less than 85 percent of their normal body weight, but are still terrified of being fat, suffer from **anorexia nervosa.** People with this disorder are usually young women who follow starvation diets and have unrealistic body images. No matter how emaciated they become, people with anorexia still think they are fat and may continue to lose weight, which can result in death. Anorexia is associated with perfectionism, excessive exercising, and an excessive desire for self-control. **Bulimia nervosa** is a more common eating disorder characterized by eating binges involving the intake of thousands of calories, followed by purging either by vomiting or using laxatives. People with this disorder are also usually young women who think obsessively about food, but who are also terrified of being fat. Following the purge, people with bulimia typically feel guilty, self-critical, and depressed. Purging can cause sore throat, swollen glands, loss of tooth enamel, nutritional deficiencies, dehydration, and intestinal damage. Results of research suggest that some people suffering this disorder secrete less cholecystokinin than normal, have a low level of serotonin, have been teased for being overweight, participate in activities that require slim bodies, have been sexually abused, or are restrained eaters.

Thirst

Regulation of thirst is similar to regulation of hunger. The lateral hypothalamus seems to be the "on" button for both hunger and thirst. When stimulated, this area of the hypothalamus will start drinking behavior, but if it is lesioned or removed, the individual refuses liquids, even to the point of dehydration. Different neurotransmitters are involved in hunger and thirst. Mouth dryness plays a minor role in stimulating us to drink. More important is the fluid content of cells and the volume of blood. Osmoreceptors are sensitive to dehydration of our cells. When osmoreceptors detect shrinking of our cells, we become thirsty. The hypothalamus stimulates the pituitary to release antidiuretic hormone (ADH), which promotes reabsorption of water in the kidneys, resulting in decreased urination. When we vomit, donate blood, or have diarrhea, the volume of our blood decreases, resulting in decreased blood pressure. This stimulates kidney cells to release an enzyme that causes synthesis of angiotensin, which stimulates thirst receptors in our hypothalamus and septum. Drinking behavior and reabsorption of water in the kidneys result. Not only is thirst affected by internal cues, but it is affected by external cues too. We often get thirsty when we see other people drinking in real life or advertisements. These external stimuli can act as an incentive that stimulates drinking behavior, even when we have had enough to drink. What we drink is affected by customs as well as the weather.

Pain Reduction

Whereas hunger and thirst drives promote eating and drinking behavior, pain promotes avoidance or escape behavior to eliminate causes of discomfort. (Additional information about pain is in Chapter 7.)

Sex

Like hunger and thirst, the sex drive involves the hypothalamus, but unlike hunger and thirst, the sex drive can be aroused by almost anything at any time and is not necessary for survival of an individual. The sex drive increases at puberty with an increase in male sex hormones, such as testosterone, and estrogen, as well as small amounts of testosterone, in females. Secretion of hormones by the hypothalamus stimulates the pituitary gland to secrete luteinizing hormone (LH) and follicle-stimulating hormone (FSH) into the bloodstream, which stimulate gonads (testes in males and ovaries in females) to secrete testosterone and estrogen that initiate and maintain arousal. Without these two hormones, sexual desire is greatly reduced in all species, but testosterone levels in humans seem related to sexual motivation in both sexes. Humans seem less instinctively driven to have children than other animals. Many learned cues are involved in this drive. Societies attempt to regulate sexual behavior by imposing sanctions against incest and encouraging or discouraging masturbation, premarital intercourse, marital intercourse, extramarital intercourse, and homosexuality.

In the 1940s, when biology professor Alfred Kinsey coordinated preparation for a marriage course, he found little scientific information available about sex and decided to pursue that research. He began to interview people about their sex histories, trained other interviewers, and founded the Institute for Sex Research, now the Kinsey Institute, at Indiana University. His popular book *Sexual Behavior in the Human Male* was based on thousands of interviews, although participants were not randomly selected. A similar book about females followed.

Sexual orientation refers to the direction of an individual's sexual interest. **Homosexuality** is a tendency to direct sexual desire toward another person of the same sex, and **bisexuality** is a tendency to direct sexual desire toward people of both sexes. **Heterosexuality** is a tendency to direct sexual desire toward people of the opposite sex. While most people are heterosexual, about 10 percent are estimated to be homosexual.

Although the sex drive is not necessary for survival of an individual, it is necessary for survival of the species. According to evolutionary psychologists, mammalian females lack incentive to mate with many males because they optimize reproductive success by being selective in mating, choosing a male who has resources to provide for children. On the other hand, males optimize reproductive success by mating with many females, choosing young, healthy, fertile females.

Masters and Johnson described a pattern of four stages in the biological **sexual response cycle** of typical men and women, including excitement characterized by sexual arousal; plateau, which involves increased breathing rate, muscle tension, heart rate, and blood pressure; orgasm, which is characterized by ejaculation in males and pleasurable sensations induced by rhythmic muscle contractions in both sexes; and resolution as blood leaves the genitals and sexual arousal lessens, followed in most males by a refractory period during which another erection or orgasm is not achieved. Females show less tendency for a refractory period and are often capable of multiple orgasms.

Social Motivation

Achievement

According to David McClelland, the **achievement motive** is a desire to meet some internalized standard of excellence. McClelland used responses to the **Thematic Apperception Test (TAT)** to measure achievement motivation. He suggested that people with a high need for achievement choose moderately challenging tasks to satisfy their need. They avoid easy goals that offer no sense of satisfaction and avoid impossible goals that offer no hope of success. People low in need for achievement select very easy or impossible goals so that they do not have to take any responsibility for failure. College students high in this need attribute success to their own ability, and attribute failure to a lack of effort. Some people fear success because success can invite envy or criticism that strains social relationships or even rejection.

Affiliation

The **affiliation motive** is the need to be with others. In general, people isolated for a long time become anxious. The affiliation motive is aroused when people feel threatened, anxious, or celebratory. According to evolutionary psychologists, social bonds provided our ancestors with both survival and reproductive benefits offering group members opportunities for food, shelter, safety, reproduction, and care of the young. Affiliation behavior involves an interaction of biological and social factors.

Intrinsic Versus Extrinsic Motivation

When you do something because you enjoy it or want to test your ability or gain skill, your motivation is usually intrinsic. Curiosity and a desire for knowledge stem from intrinsic needs. **Intrinsic motivation** is a desire to perform an activity for its own sake rather than an external reward. **Extrinsic motivation** is a desire to perform an activity to obtain a reward from outside the individual, such as money and other material goods we have learned to enjoy, such as applause or attention. Society is largely extrinsically motivated by rewards such as money. People who are intrinsically motivated by inner desires for creativity, fulfillment, and inner satisfaction tend to be psychologically healthier and happier. When people are given a reward for doing something for which they are intrinsically motivated, their intrinsic motivation often diminishes, resulting in the **overjustification effect** in which the constructs a person uses. People who use few constructs tend to stereotype others. People who use too many tend to have difficulty predicting other people's behavior.

Albert Bandura, Julian Rotter, and Walter Mischel blended behavioral and cognitive perspectives into their theories of personality that stress the interaction of thinking with learning experiences in a social environment, now called social cognitive (social-learning) theories. Although he started his career as a strict behaviorist, Albert Bandura thinks that Skinner's operant conditioning theory is inadequate to explain personality.

Albert Bandura's Social Cognitive Theory

Bandura thinks that we learn more by observational learning than by operant conditioning. He explains behavior using his concept of **reciprocal determinism,** which states that the characteristics of the person, the person's behavior, and the environment all affect one another in two-way causal relationships. The person includes personality characteristics, cognitive processes, and self-regulation skills. The person's behavior includes the nature, frequency, and intensity of actions. The environment includes stimuli from the social or physical environment and reinforcement contingencies. For example, if we are fun-loving, we select environments that we believe will be entertaining, and because we think a particular environment will be entertaining, it may impact both how we act in that environment and how we view it.

According to Bandura, self-efficacy is the major factor in how we regulate our lives. **Self-efficacy** is our belief that we can perform behaviors that are necessary to accomplish tasks, and that we are competent. When we have high self-efficacy, we think that we can master situations and produce positive results. This affects how much we are willing to take risks and try new things. Our self-efficacy can be high in one area and low in another, for example, in academics and sports. In North America and Western Europe, our societies foster an independent view of the self characterized by **individualism,** identifying oneself in terms of personal traits with independent, personal goals. Bandura has extended his theory to behavior of the individual in groups.

Collective efficacy is our perception that with collaborative effort, our group will obtain its desired outcome. Some recent research studies indicate that high self-efficacy appears to be more beneficial in individualistic societies, such as North American and Western European societies, and high collective efficacy seems to be more beneficial in collectivistic societies, such as Asian societies, for achievement of group goals. Asian countries (including Japan, China, and India) foster an interdependent view of the self characterized by **collectivism,** primary identification of an individual as a member of a group (family, school, company, community) and goals of the group as one's own goals.

Julian Rotter's Social-Learning Theory

The key concept of Julian Rotter's social learning theory is **locus of control,** the degree to which we expect that a reinforcement or outcome of our behavior is contingent on our own behavior or personal characteristics, as opposed to the degree to which we expect that a reinforcement or outcome of our behavior is a function of luck or fate, is under the control of others, or is unpredictable. Those with an internal locus of control think they control and are responsible for what happens to them—for example, their hard work gets rewarded. In contrast, those with an external locus of control believe that what happens to them is due to fate, luck, or others—for example, people get promotions because they know the right people. Our locus of control has a major impact upon our personalities because it influences both how we think about ourselves and the actions we take.

Walter Mischel's Cognitive-Affective Personality System

Walter Mischel studied with Julian Rotter, who then was Albert Bandura's colleague. Building on Rotter's and Bandura's theories, Mischel developed a cognitive-affective personality system (CAPS). According to CAPS, interaction among five factors and characteristics of the situation account for our individual differences, as well as differences in our own behavior across different situations. The five factors are our encoding strategies, our expectancies and beliefs, our goals and values, our feelings, and our personal competencies and self-regulatory processes. We develop unique **behavioral signatures,** consistent ways of responding in similar situations that characterize our personality.

Cognitive and social-learning theories are criticized for overlooking the importance of emotions in our personalities and not recognizing unconscious motivation.

Trait Theory

Trait and type theorists try to describe basic behaviors that define personality and to create instruments that measure individual differences in order to understand and predict behavior. They assume that we each have relatively stable personality characteristics or dispositional attributes, called traits or types. A **trait** is a relatively permanent characteristic of our personality that can be used to predict our behavior. Although some distinguish between traits and types by considering traits to be continuous dimensions and types to be discontinuous categories into which people fit, this distinction is not always clear. For example, Eysenck's theory can be considered either a trait or type theory because his personality types result from the interactions of trait dimensions. Important trait/type theorists include Gordon Allport, Hans Eysenck, Raymond Cattell, Paul Costa, and Robert McCrae.

Gordon Allport's Trait Theory

After meeting with Freud when he was beginning his career, Gordon Allport decided that psychoanalysis was too concerned with symbols and unconscious motivations. Allport conducted idiographic research that focused on conscious motivation and personal traits. His trait theory proposed three levels of traits. A **cardinal trait** is a defining characteristic, in a small number of us, that dominates and shapes all of our behavior. Mother Teresa is the most cited example of a person whose life focused on **altruism**—benefiting others, even to her own detriment. A **central trait** is a general characteristic, between 5 and 10 of which shape much of our behavior. For example, cheerfulness and shyness can be central traits. A *secondary trait* is a characteristic apparent in only certain situations. For example, being uncomfortable in confined spaces can be a secondary trait. Our unique pattern of traits determines our behavior.

Hans Eysenck's Personality Dimensions

Another trait/type theorist, psychologist Hans Eysenck, tried to reduce description of our personalities to three major genetically influenced dimensions, which everyone possesses to varying degrees. He used **factor analysis,** a statistical procedure that identifies common factors among groups of items, to simplify a long list of traits into his three dimensions: **extroversion** (also **extraversion**), **neuroticism,** and **psychoticism.** Extroversion measures our sociability and tendency to pay attention to the external environment, as opposed to our private mental experiences. **Neuroticism** measures our level of instability—how moody, anxious, and unreliable we are—as opposed to stability—how calm, even-tempered, and reliable we are. **Psychoticism** measures our level of tough-mindedness—how hostile, ruthless, and insensitive we are—as opposed to tender-mindedness—how friendly, empathetic, and cooperative we are. Twin studies indicate a hereditary component to these three dimensions.

Raymond Cattell's 16 Personality Factors

A trait theorist who conducted nomothetic research, Raymond Cattell, wanted to find out how traits are organized and how they are linked. Through the use of surveys and records, Cattell studied features of **surface traits,** visible areas of personality. He found that many surface traits were either absent or present in clusters in people, indicating that they represented a single more basic trait. Using factor analysis, Cattell developed a list of 16 basic traits. He considered these more basic traits **source traits,** underlying personality characteristics. Cattell's *Sixteen Personality Factor Questionnaire,* also called the 16 PF, yields trait profiles that enable psychologists to get a picture of our personality.

The Big Five Personality Factors

Many personality psychologists considered Eysenck's three dimensions to be too few to describe personality, but Cattell's 16 to be too many. More recently, trait psychologists Paul Costa and Robert McCrae have developed a five-factor model of personality, nicknamed "The Big Five." In cross-cultural studies, the same five factors have been identified in trait ratings. The Big Five Theory includes the traits of openness, conscientiousness, extraversion, agreeableness, and neuroticism.

These can be more easily remembered by using their acronym OCEAN, or CANOE.

Assessment Techniques

Psychologists use a wide variety of techniques to measure personality, including interviews, direct observation and behavioral assessment, projective tests, and personality inventories. Psychologists, human resources specialists, and others use two types of interviews that both involve obtaining information about personal history, personality traits, and current psychological state. *Unstructured interviews* involve informal conversation centered on the individual, whereas *structured interviews* involve the interviewer posing a series of planned questions that the interviewee answers. The person being interviewed provides not only verbal answers but also nonverbal information with his or her facial expressions, tone of voice, gestures, and posture. Diagnostic interviews, college interviews, and employment interviews are often structured but can be unstructured. While interviews can supply essential information about personality, they have limitations resulting from the interviewer's preconceptions, attempts at deception by the interviewee, and the halo effect. The **halo effect** is the tendency to generalize a favorable impression to unrelated dimensions of the subject's personality.

Direct Observation

Have you ever watched the behavior of people as you waited in line or sat in a public place? If so, you were engaging in a process similar to the assessment known as direct observation. Psychologists sometimes look at the behavior of an individual as he or she interacts with others, carries on normal functions, or performs specific tasks in order to identify personality traits or problems. Behaviorists prefer observational techniques. They may use rating scales that list personality traits or behaviors to be evaluated. *Behavioral assessments* record the frequency of specific behaviors in an observation. Though they criticize the subjective nature of other types of assessment, behaviorists also have to make inferences about what they see in another person's behavior. Lab studies have careful controls, but a potential flaw with naturalistic observational studies is the **Hawthorn effect.** When people know that they are being observed, they change their behavior to what they think the observer expects or to make themselves look good.

Projective Tests

Psychoanalysts use **projective personality tests** that present ambiguous stimuli, such as inkblots or pictures, with the assumption that test takers will project their unconscious thoughts or feelings onto the stimuli. The objective is to uncover deeply hidden unconscious thoughts, feelings, wishes, and needs. The famous Rorschach inkblot test presents 10 bilaterally symmetrical inkblots, asking the person to tell what he or she sees in each one and to indicate the features of the inkblot that prompted the response. The evaluator scores each response based on a rubric, inputs the data into a scoring system, and then uses clinical judgment to prepare a profile of the person's motives and conflicts. Another projective test, the Thematic Apperception Test (TAT) created by Henry Murray and Christiana Morgan, consists of a set of 20 cards (one blank) with people in ambiguous situations. People are shown a number of cards in sequence. Murray thought that people would reveal their need for achievement, sex, power, or affiliation in their answers to requests to tell what is happening in the picture, what led up to it, how the people feel, and how the situation turns out. For example, people who tell stories in which people work hard to accomplish their goals or overcome obstacles indicate a high need for achievement. Because they are unstructured, projective tests often get people to talk about anxiety-provoking situations that they otherwise wouldn't reveal, exposing unconscious conflicts. Although psychoanalysts have delineated ways to interpret the subjective responses on projective tests, other psychologists question the validity and reliability of these assessments.

Self-Reported Tests

Self-report methods, the most common personality assessment techniques, involve the person answering a series of questions, such as a personality questionnaire, or supplying information about himself or herself. Different psychologists and different approaches make use of different self-report methods. Jung's personality types are measured by the Myers–Briggs Type Indicator; Cattell's personality traits are measured by the 16 PF; Rotter's locus of control is measured by the Internal-External Locus of Control Scale; Maslow's self-actualization is measured by the Personal Orientation Inventory; Rogers's congruence between the actual self and ideal self is measured by the Q-sort. The validity of all of these is questioned. Among the best-known, most researched, and most widely used self-report personality tests is the **MMPI-2** (Minnesota Multiphasic Personality Inventory–2), composed of 567 true–false items. The items were originally chosen from among hundreds given to groups of people diagnosed with psychological disorders as well as "normal" people. Items that differentiated between the patient group and the normal group were included in the test; items that didn't were eliminated. Each item needed to correlate highly with some trait or dimension of personality. The test has 10 clinical scales such as schizophrenia and depression, 15 content scales such as anger and family problems, and validity scales to detect whether or not a person is lying. The tests are scored objectively, usually by computer, and charted as an MMPI-2 profile. Patterns of responses reveal personality dimensions. By comparing someone's profile to the profile of the normal group, psychologists identify abnormalities. Employers sometimes compare the profile of a job applicant to the profile of successful employees in making employment decisions. As well researched and carefully constructed as the MMPI-2 is, its validity is not guaranteed, and some psychologists think peer reports yield more valid information. Two assessments designed to assess personality based on the five-factor model in healthy people have been gaining in popularity: the NEO Personality Inventory (NEO-PI) and the Big Five Questionnaire (BFQ), which is being used in cross-cultural research.

Self-Concept and Self-Esteem

Our **self-concept** is our overall view of our abilities, behavior, and personality or what we know about ourselves. **Self-esteem** is one part of our self-concept, or how we *evaluate* ourselves. Our self-esteem is affected by our emotions and comes to mean how *worthy* we think we are. The self-concept is immature in youth but broadens and becomes more complex and individualized as we get older. For example, we understand that we can be attractive physically, but that we have strengths and weaknesses in many diverse areas beyond physical and mental abilities. Parents and educators can help children increase their self-worth and raise their self-esteem by highlighting the youngsters' strengths. Low self-esteem can lead to depression when a person thinks he or she is unable to realize his or her hopes, whereas it can lead to anxiety when a person thinks he or she is unable to do what he or she should.

Freud's Psychosexual Theory of Development—sequential and discontinuous stages with changing erogenous zone and conflict in each stage. If conflict is not successfully resolved, the result is fixation. The stages are the following:

- **Oral stage**—pleasure from sucking; conflict is weaning from bottle or breast; oral fixation; oral-dependent personalities are gullible, overeaters, and passive, while oral-aggressive personalities are sarcastic and argumentative.

- **Anal stage**—pleasure from holding in or letting go of feces; conflict is toilet training; anal fixation; anal-retentive personalities are orderly, obsessively neat, stingy, and stubborn; or anal-expulsive personalities are messy, disorganized, and lose their temper.

- **Phallic stage**—pleasure from self-stimulation of genitals; conflict is castration anxiety or penis envy. Healthy resolution of Oedipal/Electra complex results in identification with same-sex parent; fixation; homosexuality or relationship problems.

- **Latency stage**—suppressed sexuality; pleasure in accomplishments; if accomplishments fall short of expectations, development of feelings of inferiority.

- **Genital stage**—adolescent to adulthood; pleasure from intercourse and intimacy with another person.

Carl Jung's analytic theory emphasized the influence of our evolutionary past on our personality with the **collective unconscious**—the powerful and influential system that contains universal memories and ideas that all people have inherited from ancestors over the course of evolution.

- **Archetypes**—inherited memories or common themes found in all cultures, religions, and literature, both ancient and modern.

- **Individuation**—psychological process by which we become an individual; a unified whole, including conscious and unconscious processes.

Alfred Adler's individual or ego theory emphasized social interest as the primary determinant of personality. We strive for superiority and try to compensate for inferiority complexes.

Karen Horney attacked Freud's male bias and suggested the male counterpart for penis envy is womb envy. She thought females were more envious of the male's social status.

Humanistic approach—Humans are born good and strive for positive personal growth.

- Abraham Maslow emphasized the goal of **self-actualization**—reaching toward the best person we can be.

- Carl Rogers's self-theory or the view that the individual's self-concept is formed by society's conditions of worth and the need for **unconditional positive regard**—acceptance and love from others independent of how we behave.

Behavioral approach—According to Skinner, our history of reinforcement shapes our behavior, which is our personality.

Cognitive and social cognitive/social-learning approach—Cognitive theories say human nature is basically neutral and we are shaped by our perceptions of the world.

- George Kelly's personal construct theory looks at how we develop bipolar mental constructs to judge and predict others' behavior.

- Social cognitive/social-learning theories stress the interaction of thinking with learning experiences in a social environment.

- Albert Bandura's **reciprocal determinism** states that three types of factors all affect one another in explaining our behavior: personality characteristics and cognitive processes; the nature, frequency, and intensity of actions; stimuli from the social or physical environment, and reinforcement contingencies.

- Julian Rotter's **locus of control** is the degree to which we expect that a reinforcement or outcome of our behavior is contingent on our own behavior or personal characteristics (internal locus of control), as opposed to the degree to which we expect that a reinforcement or outcome of our behavior is a function of luck or fate, is under the control of others, or is unpredictable (external locus of control).

- Walter Mischel developed a cognitive-affective personality system (CAPS). Interaction among five factors (our encoding strategies, our expectancies and beliefs, our goals and values, our feelings, and our personal competencies and self-regulatory processes) and characteristics of the situation account for our individual differences.

Self-efficacy is our belief that we can perform behaviors that are necessary to accomplish tasks and that we are competent.

Collective efficacy is our perception that with collaborative effort our group will obtain its desired outcome. Research studies indicate high self-efficacy is more beneficial in individualistic societies and high collective efficacy in collectivistic societies for achievement of group goals.

Trait theory—A **trait** is a relatively permanent characteristic of our personality that can be used to predict our behavior.

Gordon Allport's trait theory proposed three levels of traits:

- **Cardinal trait**—defining characteristic, in a small number of us, that dominates and shapes all of our behavior.

- **Central trait**—general characteristic; between 5 and 10 of these shape much of our behavior.

- *Secondary trait*—a characteristic apparent in only certain situations. Our unique pattern of traits determines our behavior.

Hans Eysenck used three genetically influenced dimensions to describe personality. He used **factor analysis,** a statistical procedure that identifies common factors among groups of items, to determine his three dimensions:

- **Extroversion** (also **extraversion**)—measures our sociability and tendency to pay attention to the external environment, as opposed to our private mental experiences.

- **Neuroticism**—measures our level of instability—how moody, anxious, and unreliable we are—as opposed to stability—how calm, even-tempered, and reliable we are.

- **Psychoticism**—measures our level of tough-mindedness—how hostile, ruthless, and insensitive we are—as opposed to tender-mindedness—how friendly, empathetic, and cooperative we are.

Raymond Cattell studied **surface traits**—hundreds of visible areas of personality. He developed a list of 16 basic traits, **source traits,** that underlie personality characteristics. His *Sixteen Personality Factor Questionnaire* (16 PF) yields trait profiles of personality.

Paul Costa and Robert McCrae used factor analysis to identify five broad dimensions of personality. Five-factor model of personality, nicknamed "The Big Five," includes the traits of openness, conscientiousness, extraversion, agreeableness, and neuroticism.

Assessment techniques to measure personality:

- *Unstructured interviews* involve informal conversation centered on the individual.

- *Structured interviews* involve the interviewer posing a series of planned questions that the interviewee answers.

- *Behavioral assessments*—record the frequency of specific behaviors in an observation.

- Psychoanalysts use **projective personality tests**—presenting ambiguous stimuli, such as inkblots or pictures, with the assumption that test takers will project their unconscious thoughts or feelings onto the stimuli. Examples are the Rorschach inkblot test and Thematic Apperception Test (TAT).

- **Self-report methods**, the most common personality assessment techniques, involve answering a series of questions, such as a personality questionnaire, or supplying information about himself or herself.

Jung's personality types are measured by the Myers–Briggs Type Indicator.

Cattell's personality traits are measured by the 16 PF.

Rotter's locus of control is measured by the Internal–External Locus of Control Scale.

Maslow's self-actualization is measured by the Personal Orientation Inventory.

Rogers's congruence between the actual self and ideal self is measured by the Q-sort.

MMPI-2 (Minnesota Multiphasic Personality Inventory–2)—567 true-false items.

Patterns of responses reveal personality dimensions.

NEO Personality Inventory (NEO-PI) and the Big Five Questionnaire (BFQ)—assess personality based on the five-factor model in healthy people; used in cross-cultural research.

Halo effect—tendency to generalize a favorable impression to unrelated dimensions of the subject's personality.

Hawthorn effect—when people know that they are being observed, they change their behavior to what they think the observer expects or to make themselves look good.

Self-concept—our overall view of our abilities, behavior, and personality.

Self-esteem—one part of our self-concept or how we *evaluate* ourselves.

CHAPTER 12

Clinical Psychology

IN THIS CHAPTER

Summary: What is the first thing that comes to mind when you think about psychology? Before you took a psychology course, it was probably mental health, especially abnormal behavior. Actually, 90 percent of what psychologists study is about normal behavior. People in good mental health have flexible beliefs; perceptions linked to an external stimulus; logical, coherent, goal-directed thoughts; and a full range of emotions and engage readily in normal verbal communication and motor acts. Martin Seligman, a former president of the American Psychological Association, promoted the *positive psychology movement*, an emphasis on the study of human strengths, fulfillment, and optimal living to help us improve our lives. Although this movement is gaining in strength and popularity, mental health professionals are still needed to help people suffering from psychological problems.

If a close friend or family member were experiencing severe anxiety that interfered with his or her everyday life, what credentials would you want a therapist for him or her to have? This chapter looks at definitions, causes, and types of psychological disorders. It also examines how mental health practitioners approach and treat these disorders.

Key Ideas

- ✪ Defining abnormal behavior
- ✪ Causes of abnormal behavior
- ✪ Anxiety disorders
- ✪ Obsessive-compulsive and related disorders
- ✪ Trauma and stressor-related disorders
- ✪ Somatic symptom and related disorders
- ✪ Dissociative disorders
- ✪ Depressive disorders

He thought that the way to relieve the anxieties is to resolve the unconscious conflicts, which are covered by layers of experience. Psychoanalysis involves going back to discover the roots of problems, then changing one's misunderstandings and emotions after identifying the problem. His treatment plan to bring the conflict into the conscious mind, enabling the client to gain insight and achieve personality change, includes the techniques of free association and dream interpretation.

In traditional psychoanalysis, the client participates in several sessions every week for 2 or 3 years, during which the therapist sits behind the patient and asks him or her to say whatever comes to mind, called **free association.** If clients do not censor what they say, key thoughts will make unconscious conflicts accessible. Since threatening experiences and feelings can be revealed when controls of the ego and superego are relaxed during sleep, the analyst may ask the client to recall his or her dreams. The recalled dream—the surface meaning—is called the **manifest content.** The therapist works with the client to find the hidden, underlying meaning (the **latent content**), by analyzing symbols within the dream. **Hypnosis** and *Freudian slips,* Freud's "faulty actions," for which his editor/translator adopted the term *parapraxes,* may also reveal hidden conflicts. **Resistance**—blocking of anxiety-provoking feelings and experiences, evidenced by behavior such as talking about trivial issues or coming late for sessions—is a sign that the client has reached an important issue that needs to be discovered. Although the analyst's behavior is neutral, the client may respond to the analyst as though he or she is a significant person in the client's emotional life. Known as **transference,** this behavior can allow the client to replay previous experiences and reactions, enabling him or her to gain insight about current feelings and behaviors. **Catharsis,** the release of emotional tension after remembering or reliving an emotionally charged experience from the past, may ultimately result in relief of anxiety. Traditional psychoanalysis requires too much time and is too expensive for the vast majority of people seeking help.

Psychodynamic and Interpersonal Psychotherapy

Psychoanalytic theory influences modern *psychodynamic psychotherapy,* which is typically shorter in duration, less frequent, and involves the client sitting up and talking to the therapist. The more active therapist is likely to point out and interpret relevant associations and help the client uncover unresolved conflict more directly to gain insight into the problem and work through feelings. Although psychodynamic therapists think that anxieties are rooted in past experiences, they do not necessarily assume the problems arose in infancy and early childhood.

Even shorter *interpersonal psychotherapy* aims to enable people to gain insight into the causes of their problems, but it focuses on current relations to relieve present symptoms.

Humanistic Therapies

Humanistic therapies include client-centered or person-centered therapies, and Gestalt therapy. Humanists think that problems arise because the client's inherent goodness and potential to grow emotionally have been stifled by external psychosocial constraints. The goal of client-centered therapy is to provide an atmosphere of acceptance (**unconditional positive regard**), understanding (*empathy*), and sharing that permits the client's inner strength and qualities to surface so that personal growth can occur and problems can be eliminated, ultimately resulting in **self-actualization.** According to humanist Carl Rogers, the greater the difference between the **ideal self** and the **real self,** the greater the problems of the client. His emphasis on developing a more positive self-concept through **unconditional positive regard, active listening,** and showing both sensitivity and genuineness is a central focus of nondirective Rogerian psychotherapy. Nondirective therapy encourages the client to take the lead in determining the direction of therapy. Rogers's technique of **active listening** involves echoing, restating, and seeking clarification of what the client says and does and acknowledging feelings.

Influenced by Gestalt psychology, which emphasized that people organize their view of the world to make meaning, psychoanalyst Fritz Perls said that people create their own reality and continue to grow psychologically only as long as they perceive, stay aware of, and act on their true feelings. He developed **Gestalt therapy.** The therapist's goal is to push clients to decide whether they will allow past conflicts to control their future or whether they will choose right now to take control of their own destiny. In contrast to client-centered therapy, Gestalt therapists are directive in questioning and challenge clients to help them become aware of their feelings and problems, and to discard feelings and values that are not their own. Similar to psychoanalysts, Gestalt therapists use dream interpretation to help the client gain a better understanding of the whole self. Through role playing, the therapist gets the client to express his or her true feelings. Like other humanistic therapies, the emphasis is on present behavior, feelings, and thoughts to get the client aware of how these factors interact to affect his or her whole being.

Insight therapies have been demonstrated to be effective for treating eating disorders, depressive disorders, and marital discord.

Behavioral Approaches

B. F. Skinner and other behaviorists discount the insight therapies. To Skinner, abnormal behavior is a result of maladaptive behavior learned through faulty rewards and punishment. The goal of **behavior therapy** is to extinguish unwanted behavior and replace it with more adaptive behavior. Therapies are based on the learning principles of classical conditioning, operant conditioning, and observational or social learning theory.

Classical Conditioning Therapies

After Watson conditioned Baby Albert to fear a rat, he planned to remove the fear, but Albert was taken away. Soon thereafter, Mary Cover Jones worked with a young child who feared white rabbits, rats, and similar stimuli. Over several months, she gradually introduced a rabbit closer and closer to the child while he ate and played. The boy's fear was gradually eliminated. Joseph Wolpe dubbed her "the mother of behavior therapy."

Classical conditioning therapies involving reconditioning include the counterconditioning techniques of systematic desensitization, flooding, and aversive conditioning.

- Originally called *reciprocal inhibition,* **systematic desensitization** is a behavior therapy founded on the idea that an anxiety response is inhibited by an incompatible relaxation response. Joseph Wolpe explained systematic desensitization as reconditioning so that the crucial conditioned stimulus elicits the new conditioned response. The procedure has three steps. First, the client is taught progressive relaxation. Next, the therapist and client create an **anxiety hierarchy** of all associated fears from the least-feared to the most-feared stimulus. For example, for school phobia, they may list the following situations: thinking about going to school, seeing a picture of the school, getting on the school bus, walking toward the school, opening the school door, and finally sitting in the classroom. Third, the therapist has the student imagine each of the fearful associations beginning with the least-feared stimulus, the mere thought of going to school, and pairs it with relaxation. After the student can relax with this fear, the process is repeated, finally ascending to the most fear-provoking stimulus of actually sitting in the classroom. When the student can sit in the classroom and be completely relaxed, the relaxation response is effective for inhibiting the fear response. Systematic desensitization is typically accomplished within 10 sessions.

- **Flooding** is an *exposure technique,* another classical conditioning treatment for phobias and other anxiety disorders, that extinguishes the conditioned response. As a result of the client directly confronting the anxiety-provoking stimulus, extinction is achieved; the feared stimulus (the conditioned stimulus) is repeatedly presented without the reason for being afraid (the unconditioned stimulus). For example, if someone afraid of dogs is repeatedly exposed to friendly dogs that do not bite, the fear associated with the dogs will eventually be extinguished.
- Yet another form of behavior therapy based on the principles of classical conditioning, **aversive conditioning,** trains the client to associate physical or psychological discomfort with behaviors, thoughts, or situations he or she wants to stop or avoid. One example of aversive conditioning uses a drug called Antabuse (US) to discourage the use of alcohol. By itself, the drug has no chemical effect, but when paired with alcohol (CS), the combination causes extreme nausea (CR). Similar to taste aversions discussed in Chapter 8, after very few pairings of Antabuse and alcohol, the client learns to avoid alcohol. Without an occasional pairing of the Antabuse with the alcohol again, this new response can easily be extinguished.

Operant Conditioning Therapies

Operant conditioning therapies include *contingency management* techniques of behavior modification and token economies designed to change behavior by modifying its consequences. In both, rewards are used to reinforce target behaviors.

- In **behavior modification,** the client selects a goal and, with each step toward it, receives a small reward until the intended goal is finally achieved.
- In **token economies,** positive behaviors are rewarded with **secondary reinforcers** (tokens, points, etc.), which can eventually be exchanged for extrinsic rewards, such as food. Token economies are often used in institutions to encourage socially acceptable behaviors and to discourage socially unacceptable ones.

Other Behavior Therapies

Social skills training is a behavior therapy, based on operant conditioning and Albert Bandura's social learning theory, to improve interpersonal skills by using modeling, behavioral rehearsal, and shaping. With **modeling,** the client is encouraged to observe socially skilled people in order to learn appropriate behaviors. In *behavioral rehearsal,* the client practices the appropriate social behaviors through role-playing in structured situations. The therapist helps the client by providing positive reinforcement and corrective feedback. **Shaping** involves reinforcement of more and more complex social situations. Through social skills training, people with social phobias learn to make friends or date, and former mental patients learn to deal normally with people outside of the hospital.

Biofeedback training is a widely used behavioral therapy that involves giving the individual immediate information about the degree to which he or she is able to change anxiety-related responses such as heart rate, muscle tension, and skin temperature to facilitate improved control of the physiological process and, therefore, lessen physiological arousal.

Behavior therapies have been found effective for treating anxiety disorders (generalized anxiety disorder, panic disorder), obsessive-compulsive disorder, post-traumatic stress disorder, alcohol and drug addictions, bed-wetting, sexual dysfunctions, and autism spectrum disorder.

Psychoanalysts discount the quick cure offered by behaviorists. Since behaviorists are unconcerned with the cause of anxiety, analysts believe that it will resurface in a new form. Until the unconscious conflict is made conscious, the behaviorist is only "curing" the symptom of the problem; so through symptom substitution, a new problem will occur. The so-called *cured* smoker suddenly begins another compulsive habit, like eating or drinking.

Cognitive-Behavioral Approaches

Cognitive therapists, sometimes called cognitive-behavioral therapists, think that abnormal behavior is the result of faulty thought patterns. Many psychologists consider cognitive therapy to be an insight therapy. Cognitive-behavior therapy helps clients change both the way they think and the way they behave. Through **cognitive restructuring,** or turning the faulty, disordered thoughts into more realistic thoughts, the client may change abnormal behavior.

Rational Emotive Behavior Therapy

Albert Ellis developed **Rational Emotive Therapy** (RET), which is also called *rational emotive behavior therapy* (REBT), based on the idea that anxiety, guilt, depression, and other psychological problems result from self-defeating thoughts. The therapist has the client confront irrational thoughts by discussing his or her **a**ctions, his or her **b**eliefs about those actions, and finally the **c**onsequences of those beliefs. The actions, beliefs, and consequences he called the ABCs of treatment. For instance, a young man is feeling guilty about not having helped his mother more before she died. Ellis might have confronted this guilty belief with a statement like "And you were the only person in the entire universe who could have helped her, right?" While defending these beliefs, the client may see how absurd they truly are. Ellis believed that much of this thinking involves the tyranny of the "shoulds," what we believe we must do, rather than what is actually realistic or necessary.

Cognitive Triad Therapy

Aaron Beck also developed a cognitive therapy to alleviate faulty and negative thoughts. His **cognitive triad** looks at what a person thinks about his or her self, his or her world, and his or her future. Depressed individuals tend to have negative perceptions in all three areas. As noted by Martin Seligman, depressed individuals tend to think they caused the negative events, the negative events will affect everything they do, and the negative events will last forever. Such thoughts and beliefs lead to low self-esteem, depression, and anxiety. The goal of therapy is to help them change these irrationally negative beliefs into more positive and realistic views so that failures are attributed to things outside their control and successes are seen as personal accomplishments. Beck suggests specific tactics, including evaluating the evidence the client has for and against automatic thoughts, reattributing the blame to situational factors rather than the client's incompetence, and discussing alternative solutions to the problem. For example, instead of blaming yourself for being stupid when the entire class does poorly on a math exam, you might substitute the thought that you didn't have an adequate opportunity to study and that the test may not have been valid.

Cognitive therapies have been demonstrated to be effective in treating depressive disorders, eating disorders, chronic pain, marital discord, and anxiety disorders (generalized anxiety disorder, panic disorder, agoraphobia, and social phobia).

Biological/Biomedical Treatments

Biological psychologists believe that abnormal behavior results from neurochemical imbalances, abnormalities in brain structures, or possibly some genetic predisposition. Treatments, therefore, include **psychopharmacotherapy** (the use of psychotropic drugs to treat mental disorders), electroconvulsive therapy, and psychosurgery. Medical doctors, schizotypal), dramatic/emotionally problematic (including histrionic, narcissistic, borderline, and antisocial), and chronic fearfulness/avoidant (including avoidant, dependent, and obsessive-compulsive).

- **Neurodevelopmental disorders** involve disturbances in learning, language, and motor or social skills showing up in infancy, childhood, or adolescence. Neurodevelopmental disorders include intellectual disability, attention-deficit/hyperactivity disorder (ADHD), and autism spectrum disorder.

   Attention-deficit/hyperactivity (ADHD)—characterized by the inability to focus attention, distractibility, and impulsivity.

   Autism spectrum disorder—characterized by impaired social interaction, poor communication, and limited activities and interests.

Professionals who treat people with psychopathologies include the following:

- **Psychiatrists**—medical doctors (MD); can prescribe medication and perform surgery.

- **Clinical psychologists**—have doctoral degrees (PhD or PsyD); use different therapeutic approaches depending on training and diagnosis.

- **Counseling psychologists**—have PhD, EdD, PsyD, or MA in counseling; tend to deal with less severe mental health problems.

- **Psychoanalysts**—may or may not be psychiatrists, but follow the teaching of Freud and practice psychoanalysis or other psychodynamic therapies.

- **Clinical or psychiatric social workers**—typically have earned a master's degree or doctoral degree in social work (MSW or DSW), which includes a supervised internship, and have passed a certification exam.

CHAPTER 13

Social Psychology

IN THIS CHAPTER

Summary: If you could spare a few minutes for a close friend who asked for some help, would you? Of course you would. How other people, groups, and cultures shape our perceptions, attitudes, and behavior is the study of **social psychology**. It looks at how social and situational factors can influence us in both positive and negative ways. Research by **social psychologists** has raised important ethical questions because of the use of deception and manipulation to get results that are as accurate as possible. The American Psychological Association's ethical guidelines have tightened the reins on researchers as a result of some of the more controversial, yet important findings in this field.

This chapter deals with how groups affect the individual, how we perceive others and others perceive us, and how groups can affect attitude change.

Key Ideas
- ✪ Group dynamics
- ✪ Bystander intervention
- ✪ Attribution processes
- ✪ Interpersonal perception
- ✪ Conformity, compliance, and obedience
- ✪ Attitudes and attitude change
- ✪ Aggression and antisocial behavior
- ✪ Altruism
- ✪ Attraction

Group Dynamics

Humans have a basic drive to form social bonds with others. A **social group** is two or more individuals sharing common goals and interests, interacting, and influencing each other's behavior. People occupying an elevator together are not a social group, but members of a Girl Scout troop would be because they have a pattern of socializing and working together on projects and common goals. **Norms** are implicit or explicit rules that apply to all members of the group and govern acceptable behavior and attitudes. Norms allow for smooth social interactions because they let people know how they are supposed to behave. Violating these norms can be grounds for exclusion from the group, so the desire to belong will cause some members to act very differently from the way they do when they are alone. Please see Table 13.1 for an overview of all the studies discussed in this chapter.

Social Roles

Certain social **roles** or social positions are also characteristic of group membership. In the **Zimbardo prison study,** Stanford students were arbitrarily assigned the roles of either prisoner or guard. As a consequence of their role assignment, individual behavior changed dramatically in a matter of hours. Although they were well aware that the "prison" was a simulated situation, by the sixth day the experiment had to be halted because of the severe stress inflicted by certain "sadistic" guards who took their roles too seriously. The entire experiment was videotaped, and experts in the prison system were amazed at how realistic the simulated situation had become in such a short period. Those assigned the role of prisoner were cowering in their cells, and one-third of those assigned the role of guard inflicted harsh punishment for the slightest infraction of the rules.

Working together in group situations either in the classroom or in the workplace is a common practice. Certain group members, either by assignment or natural inclination, assume leadership roles while others contribute to the group effort in other ways. All too often, a group member assumes the role of "slacker." This tendency toward **social loafing** is a result of feeling less pressure to put forth effort when engaged in projects where group evaluations are being made. The "slackers" will leave the work to others who are more personally invested in always doing a good job. These same students or "slackers" tend to exert more effort if they believe they will be evaluated individually. Teachers and employers could ease group tensions by keeping this tendency in mind.

Another phenomenon that arises when people are in large groups is **deindividuation.** When we are in a large group, we tend to lose some self-awareness. We may engage in behavior that is unusual or uncharacteristic for us because of this group anonymity. This especially occurs when there is a heightened sense of arousal. Antisocial behavior from normally well-behaved individuals may occur in these situations. Let a pitcher hit a batter with a ball for a second time and watch the benches of both teams empty and a fistfight take place. This normative behavior reduces the conflict any one person feels toward acting in such a brutal way. None of the players gives much thought to the repercussions. Similarly, when a blackout occurs, we have become accustomed to expect certain groups to riot and loot. Deindividuation can also lead to prosocial behavior, with an unusual outpouring of generosity among virtual strangers all caught up in an emotionally arousing situation.

Effects of the Group

Your performance on certain tasks is also affected by being in a group situation. **Social facilitation** refers to a tendency to perform well-learned tasks better in front of others. The well-rehearsed piano student may perform much better at the recital than he or she has all week during practice. This tendency for improved performance can be explained by the

Table 13.1 Overview of Social Psychological Experiments

Experimenter(s)	Brief Description of Experiment	Results	Key Concept
Milgram	Teacher to apply electric shocks when learner does not answer questions correctly	66 percent of participants delivered what they thought to be a maximum of 450 volts	Obedience to authority
Asch	Select the line in a triad that matches the stimulus line	Subjects conformed 1/3 of the time when the confederates voted unanimously	Conformity Normative influence Social influence
Festinger	Gave two different groups either $1 or $20 to lie about a boring task to future subjects	$1 group changed their perception of the task from boring to interesting	Cognitive dissonance
Latané and Darley	Emergency situation created to test people's helping behavior	People help when they think they are alone, but the larger the group present, the less likely anyone is to act	Diffusion of responsibility Bystander intervention
Sherif	Boys' camp study where an emergency situation required group cooperation	Two previously competitive groups worked together to solve problem	Contact theory Superordinate goal
Aronson and Gonzales	Devised a teaching strategy (jigsaw) making Anglo and Latino children interdependent upon each other	Raised self-efficacy of minority children and reduced prejudice on part of Anglo children	Jigsaw classroom
Rosenthal and Jacobsen	Teachers were told prior to school year to expect certain students to "bloom" academically during the year	Teacher expectations did come true—bloomers did prove more successful than nonbloomers	Self-fulfilling prophecy
Zimbardo	Simulate a prison setting at Stanford U and assign roles of "prisoners" and "guards" to students	Simulation cut off in 6 days because of sadistic guards and ethical violations	Social roles
Triplett	Looked at the effect of an audience when learners had learned task well or were just beginning to learn it	Well-learned tasks were enhanced by audience and newly learned tasks were impaired when audience was present	Social facilitation Social impairment

level of arousal and increased motivation that occurs in front of the audience. Studies have also shown that when first learning a new task, performing in front of others leads to the opposite tendency or **social impairment.** Someone just learning to play tennis may begin to hit the ball across the net much more consistently until a crowd gathers to watch, and then the player blows nearly every shot.

STEP 5

Build Your Test-Taking Confidence

AP Psychology Practice Exam 1
AP Psychology Practice Exam 2

AP Psychology Practice Exam 1

ANSWER SHEET FOR MULTIPLE-CHOICE QUESTIONS

1 Ⓐ Ⓑ Ⓒ Ⓓ Ⓔ
2 Ⓐ Ⓑ Ⓒ Ⓓ Ⓔ
3 Ⓐ Ⓑ Ⓒ Ⓓ Ⓔ
4 Ⓐ Ⓑ Ⓒ Ⓓ Ⓔ
5 Ⓐ Ⓑ Ⓒ Ⓓ Ⓔ
6 Ⓐ Ⓑ Ⓒ Ⓓ Ⓔ
7 Ⓐ Ⓑ Ⓒ Ⓓ Ⓔ
8 Ⓐ Ⓑ Ⓒ Ⓓ Ⓔ
9 Ⓐ Ⓑ Ⓒ Ⓓ Ⓔ
10 Ⓐ Ⓑ Ⓒ Ⓓ Ⓔ
11 Ⓐ Ⓑ Ⓒ Ⓓ Ⓔ
12 Ⓐ Ⓑ Ⓒ Ⓓ Ⓔ
13 Ⓐ Ⓑ Ⓒ Ⓓ Ⓔ
14 Ⓐ Ⓑ Ⓒ Ⓓ Ⓔ
15 Ⓐ Ⓑ Ⓒ Ⓓ Ⓔ
16 Ⓐ Ⓑ Ⓒ Ⓓ Ⓔ
17 Ⓐ Ⓑ Ⓒ Ⓓ Ⓔ
18 Ⓐ Ⓑ Ⓒ Ⓓ Ⓔ
19 Ⓐ Ⓑ Ⓒ Ⓓ Ⓔ
20 Ⓐ Ⓑ Ⓒ Ⓓ Ⓔ
21 Ⓐ Ⓑ Ⓒ Ⓓ Ⓔ
22 Ⓐ Ⓑ Ⓒ Ⓓ Ⓔ
23 Ⓐ Ⓑ Ⓒ Ⓓ Ⓔ
24 Ⓐ Ⓑ Ⓒ Ⓓ Ⓔ
25 Ⓐ Ⓑ Ⓒ Ⓓ Ⓔ
26 Ⓐ Ⓑ Ⓒ Ⓓ Ⓔ
27 Ⓐ Ⓑ Ⓒ Ⓓ Ⓔ
28 Ⓐ Ⓑ Ⓒ Ⓓ Ⓔ
29 Ⓐ Ⓑ Ⓒ Ⓓ Ⓔ
30 Ⓐ Ⓑ Ⓒ Ⓓ Ⓔ
31 Ⓐ Ⓑ Ⓒ Ⓓ Ⓔ
32 Ⓐ Ⓑ Ⓒ Ⓓ Ⓔ
33 Ⓐ Ⓑ Ⓒ Ⓓ Ⓔ
34 Ⓐ Ⓑ Ⓒ Ⓓ Ⓔ
35 Ⓐ Ⓑ Ⓒ Ⓓ Ⓔ

36 Ⓐ Ⓑ Ⓒ Ⓓ Ⓔ
37 Ⓐ Ⓑ Ⓒ Ⓓ Ⓔ
38 Ⓐ Ⓑ Ⓒ Ⓓ Ⓔ
39 Ⓐ Ⓑ Ⓒ Ⓓ Ⓔ
40 Ⓐ Ⓑ Ⓒ Ⓓ Ⓔ
41 Ⓐ Ⓑ Ⓒ Ⓓ Ⓔ
42 Ⓐ Ⓑ Ⓒ Ⓓ Ⓔ
43 Ⓐ Ⓑ Ⓒ Ⓓ Ⓔ
44 Ⓐ Ⓑ Ⓒ Ⓓ Ⓔ
45 Ⓐ Ⓑ Ⓒ Ⓓ Ⓔ
46 Ⓐ Ⓑ Ⓒ Ⓓ Ⓔ
47 Ⓐ Ⓑ Ⓒ Ⓓ Ⓔ
48 Ⓐ Ⓑ Ⓒ Ⓓ Ⓔ
49 Ⓐ Ⓑ Ⓒ Ⓓ Ⓔ
50 Ⓐ Ⓑ Ⓒ Ⓓ Ⓔ
51 Ⓐ Ⓑ Ⓒ Ⓓ Ⓔ
52 Ⓐ Ⓑ Ⓒ Ⓓ Ⓔ
53 Ⓐ Ⓑ Ⓒ Ⓓ Ⓔ
54 Ⓐ Ⓑ Ⓒ Ⓓ Ⓔ
55 Ⓐ Ⓑ Ⓒ Ⓓ Ⓔ
56 Ⓐ Ⓑ Ⓒ Ⓓ Ⓔ
57 Ⓐ Ⓑ Ⓒ Ⓓ Ⓔ
58 Ⓐ Ⓑ Ⓒ Ⓓ Ⓔ
59 Ⓐ Ⓑ Ⓒ Ⓓ Ⓔ
60 Ⓐ Ⓑ Ⓒ Ⓓ Ⓔ
61 Ⓐ Ⓑ Ⓒ Ⓓ Ⓔ
62 Ⓐ Ⓑ Ⓒ Ⓓ Ⓔ
63 Ⓐ Ⓑ Ⓒ Ⓓ Ⓔ
64 Ⓐ Ⓑ Ⓒ Ⓓ Ⓔ
65 Ⓐ Ⓑ Ⓒ Ⓓ Ⓔ
66 Ⓐ Ⓑ Ⓒ Ⓓ Ⓔ
67 Ⓐ Ⓑ Ⓒ Ⓓ Ⓔ
68 Ⓐ Ⓑ Ⓒ Ⓓ Ⓔ
69 Ⓐ Ⓑ Ⓒ Ⓓ Ⓔ
70 Ⓐ Ⓑ Ⓒ Ⓓ Ⓔ

71 Ⓐ Ⓑ Ⓒ Ⓓ Ⓔ
72 Ⓐ Ⓑ Ⓒ Ⓓ Ⓔ
73 Ⓐ Ⓑ Ⓒ Ⓓ Ⓔ
74 Ⓐ Ⓑ Ⓒ Ⓓ Ⓔ
75 Ⓐ Ⓑ Ⓒ Ⓓ Ⓔ
76 Ⓐ Ⓑ Ⓒ Ⓓ Ⓔ
77 Ⓐ Ⓑ Ⓒ Ⓓ Ⓔ
78 Ⓐ Ⓑ Ⓒ Ⓓ Ⓔ
79 Ⓐ Ⓑ Ⓒ Ⓓ Ⓔ
80 Ⓐ Ⓑ Ⓒ Ⓓ Ⓔ
81 Ⓐ Ⓑ Ⓒ Ⓓ Ⓔ
82 Ⓐ Ⓑ Ⓒ Ⓓ Ⓔ
83 Ⓐ Ⓑ Ⓒ Ⓓ Ⓔ
84 Ⓐ Ⓑ Ⓒ Ⓓ Ⓔ
85 Ⓐ Ⓑ Ⓒ Ⓓ Ⓔ
86 Ⓐ Ⓑ Ⓒ Ⓓ Ⓔ
87 Ⓐ Ⓑ Ⓒ Ⓓ Ⓔ
88 Ⓐ Ⓑ Ⓒ Ⓓ Ⓔ
89 Ⓐ Ⓑ Ⓒ Ⓓ Ⓔ
90 Ⓐ Ⓑ Ⓒ Ⓓ Ⓔ
91 Ⓐ Ⓑ Ⓒ Ⓓ Ⓔ
92 Ⓐ Ⓑ Ⓒ Ⓓ Ⓔ
93 Ⓐ Ⓑ Ⓒ Ⓓ Ⓔ
94 Ⓐ Ⓑ Ⓒ Ⓓ Ⓔ
95 Ⓐ Ⓑ Ⓒ Ⓓ Ⓔ
96 Ⓐ Ⓑ Ⓒ Ⓓ Ⓔ
97 Ⓐ Ⓑ Ⓒ Ⓓ Ⓔ
98 Ⓐ Ⓑ Ⓒ Ⓓ Ⓔ
99 Ⓐ Ⓑ Ⓒ Ⓓ Ⓔ
100 Ⓐ Ⓑ Ⓒ Ⓓ Ⓔ

SECTION II

Time—50 minutes

Directions: Take approximately 50 minutes to answer *both* of the essay questions. According to the College Board directions, "It is not enough to answer a question by merely listing facts. You should present a cogent argument based on your critical analysis of the question posed, using appropriate psychological terminology." Write your essays on separate sheets of paper.

Essay 1:

For each of the pairs of terms below, provide an example of how the first term in each pair affects or is related to the second.

- Basal metabolic rate . . . . . obesity
- Spacing effect . . . . . studying
- Industrial/organizational psychology . . . . . product design
- Chameleon effect . . . . . mirror neurons
- Maturation . . . . . infant memory

Essay 2:

A neuroscientist thinks he has developed a drug that can stop the progression of Alzheimer's disease in people who are in the initial stages of the disease. Design a research experiment that will support or refute his hypothesis. In your research design describe the following:

- sample
- assignment
- independent variable
- dependent variable
- experimental group
- control group
- possible confounding variable
- how you would determine whether or not the drug is effective

END OF PRACTICE EXAM

› Answers and Explanations

Section 1

1. **A**—(Chapter 7) Olfactory (smell) receptors in the nasal passages would detect the gas molecules and send impulses directly to the brain for fast perception and response.

2. **A**—(Chapter 10) Identical twins. Since they share the same genes, the differences between them would be a result of nurture. Identical quadruplets would be extremely rare, and so it would be difficult to find a large enough sample size for a study.

3. **C**—(Chapter 8) The children's more aggressive behavior following the more violent cartoon supports Albert Bandura's social learning theory of aggression studied in the bobo doll study.

4. **C**—(Chapter 9) A phoneme is the basic unit of sound, such as *d, o, g*, which are three phonemes that together make the word *dog*. Phonemes, on their own, may not have any meaning, whereas a morpheme is the smallest unit of language that has meaning. The word *a* is both a morpheme and a phoneme.

5. **E**—(Chapter 12) Systematic desensitization is a behavior therapy especially effective in the treatment of phobias such as claustrophobia in this question. The patient learns through classical conditioning to replace the fear with relaxation.

6. **D**—(Chapter 11) A drive is a psychological state in which a person is aroused and motivated. A need is a physiological necessity, such as thirst or hunger.

7. **A**—(Chapter 11) The Rorschach inkblot test is a projective test designed to reveal the unconscious mind and is a technique quite useful to the psychoanalytic therapist.

8. **A**—(Chapter 8) When the pigeon sees the yellow light instead of the green one, he generalizes his pecking response to a similar stimulus. The pigeon can be taught to discriminate between the two colored lights but has not yet been trained to do so.

9. **C**—(Chapter 6) Carl Jung proposed that the collective unconscious is derived from ancestral memories and experiences and is common to all humankind, not just an individual.

10. **B**—(Chapter 7) The threshold is the minimum level of stimulation necessary to start a neural impulse. The neural impulse is also referred to as the action potential.

11. **A**—(Chapter 12) Joey seems to have antisocial personality disorder. He shows no guilt when he hurts others. The condition is first evident in teen years, as in this case, and the criminal behavior often accelerates over time.

12. **D**—(Chapter 8) Modeling is a social cognitive process in which new behavior is learned by watching others and then imitating their actions.

13. **D**—(Chapter 11) Freud's superego operates on the morality principle and, thus, overrides the impulse to cut class in this example and causes Andy to do the right thing by attending class.

14. **D**—(Chapter 9) Although largely discredited, Whorf believed that language determines the way we think. He cited studies of bilingual people who said that they experienced a different sense of self when thinking in two different languages.

15. **C**—(Chapter 11) A lesion in the ventromedial hypothalamus would cause a rat to continue to eat. It is theorized to be the "satiety" center, or off button, for hunger sensation, so if it were lesioned, the rat would continue to eat as long as the food supply was available.

16. **A**—(Chapter 13) Prejudice is the unjustifiable negative attitude toward a group and its members, while discrimination would be acting upon this attitude.

17. **C**—(Chapter 12) One technique used by Carl Rogers in his client-centered humanistic therapy is to give unconditional positive regard to his clients to undo the effects of conditions of worth and to allow the individual to realize his or her positive actualizing potential.

18. **D**—(Chapter 13) People dressed alike or disguised can easily lose their sense of identity and become less self-aware, which are characteristics of deindividuation.

19. **D**—(Chapter 10) Piaget's formal operational thought is the final stage of reasoning, characterized

by hypothetical thought, systematic planning, and abstract, logical reasoning abilities.

20. **B**—(Chapter 6) In patients with Parkinson's disease, damage occurs in the dopamine-rich substantia nigra. With the degeneration of these neurons, movement problems begin to occur. A synthetic drug known as L-dopa is able to alleviate some of their movement problems. Symptoms of schizophrenia are related to an excessive amount of dopamine.

21. **B**—(Chapter 5) Watson and Raynor's classic study involving classical conditioning of fear in 9-month-old baby Albert would today violate the APA ethical guidelines that prohibit physical or mental suffering by subjects.

22. **D**—(Chapter 11) According to Maslow's Hierarchy of Needs, the base consists of one's physiological needs, followed by safety, belongingness and love, esteem, self-actualization, and self-transcendence, respectively.

23. **D**—(Chapter 12) Brenda's constant attention-seeking and egotistical attitudes are classic markers of the narcissistic personality.

24. **C**—(Chapter 5) Behaviorists discount the role of "mentalistic" aspects that cannot be directly observed.

25. **E**—(Chapter 11) According to Erik Erikson, when children gain pleasure from applying themselves to certain tasks, they are feeling a sense of industry. Those who do not derive pleasure from applying themselves may feel inferior.

26. **C**—(Chapter 7) The height of the wave or its amplitude allows us to perceive loudness from sound waves.

27. **B**—(Chapter 9) Shannon's inability to think of using her jeans and sweater as a pillow is an example of functional fixedness—not seeing unusual uses for familiar objects.

28. **A**—(Chapter 11) Karen Horney disagreed with Freud's assumption that all women have weak superegos and experience "penis envy." She founded feminist psychology and believed the differences between men and women are biological, not psychological.

29. **A**—(Chapter 11) The MMPI-2 is the most widely used self-report inventory for personality assessment.

30. **C**—(Chapter 12) Behaviorists believe that we learn new behavior through rewards and punishment. Any maladaptive behavior can be changed by altering the consequences of that behavior.

31. **D**—(Chapter 9) Insight learning is the sudden appearance of a solution when directed thinking is no longer being utilized. As Scott consciously shifted his attention to other matters, the solution to the anagram came to him.

32. **A**—(Chapter 12) People with schizophrenia suffer from disordered thinking and often have delusions of persecution and hallucinations.

33. **A**—(Chapter 5) Jyoti is utilizing the naturalistic observation technique frequently used by behaviorists.

34. **B**—(Chapter 7) White is the appearance of reflected wavelengths of all colors.

35. **C**—(Chapter 9) Used on the old Stanford–Binet intelligence tests, the Intelligence Quotient originally coined by William Stearns represents your mental age divided by your chronological age multiplied by 100. Your mental age is a measure of your intellectual development relative to others.

36. **D**—(Chapter 10) Kübler-Ross's classic study of 200 terminal cancer patients determined their emotional reactions followed a similar pattern. Denial is followed by the emotions of anger, bargaining, depression, and acceptance.

37. **C**—(Chapter 6) The sympathetic nervous system is the part of the autonomic nervous system activated in stressful situations. When Jared realizes the shadows are just that, the parasympathetic nervous system will be activated to return his body to homeostasis.

38. **E**—(Chapter 6) Narcotics or opiates are the classification of drugs most used to relieve patients' pain. Because they are highly addictive, a doctor must prescribe their limited use.

39. **A**—(Chapter 12) One of the characteristics of the manic high is an inflated ego and sense of euphoria. The patient has little need for sleep during this phase of the condition.

40. **A**—(Chapter 9) According to the serial positioning effect, words at the beginning of the list are stored in your long-term memory. Words remembered at the end of the list are in your

short-term memory, which lasts only 20+ seconds and would be forgotten 2 days later. Poorest recall would occur for words in the middle of the list.

41. **A**—(Chapter 11) Tony's sense of self-efficacy or belief in his abilities to accomplish tasks should be maximized by all of these accomplishments.

42. **B**—(Chapter 11) Fixed-action patterns are species-specific innate behaviors unaffected by learning.

43. **B**—(Chapter 9) To standardize a test, each of the actions mentioned would be taken—pretesting of a sample population for whom the test is intended under uniform instructions.

44. **B**—(Chapter 12) Compulsive hand washing is a common experience of those suffering from obsessive-compulsive disorder. A compulsion is the repetition of some action over and over even though it serves no useful purpose.

45. **D**—(Chapter 5) The survey technique is being utilized here. It is a research method that obtains large samples of responses through questionnaire or interview. No variables have been manipulated as in an experiment.

46. **C**—(Chapter 7) Sensory adaptation is the lessening of perception of a stimulus with repeated stimulation, like the temperature of the pool water. You perceive the pool water as cold when you first jump in, but the neural firing decreases over time with repeated stimulation and you no longer notice it.

47. **E**—(Chapter 12) *DSM-5* is a diagnostic guide used by mental health professionals to diagnose patients. It lists symptoms of these disorders, but does not list the causes of mental disorders.

48. **C**—(Chapter 11) According to set point theory, an individual's regulated weight is balanced by adjusting food intake and metabolic rate.

49. **C**—(Chapter 6) Only the PET scan images function of the brain. The CAT and MRI both show the structures of the brain in good detail. The fMRI, like the PET, can show both structure and function.

50. **A**—(Chapter 12) To have been diagnosed with schizophrenia, Aaron would have had to have a

break with reality and may have been unable to tell the difference between right and wrong. A person who is legally insane during the commission of acts constituting an offense is unable to appreciate the nature and quality, or the wrongfulness, of his acts. According to law, "Mental disease or defect does not otherwise constitute a defense."

51. **C**—(Chapter 13) Group A is likely to become more entrenched. This is an example of group polarization.

52. **C**—(Chapter 10) Penfield's studies suggest that the old memories are still present and probably have not been stimulated or needed to be retrieved recently.

53. **B**—(Chapter 11) Displacement, a Freudian defense mechanism, allows us to express feelings toward a group or individual perceived to be less threatening to us, rather than the direct target or ourselves.

54. **D**—(Chapter 10) Longitudinal studies follow the same group of people for a longer time. They are tested at several points, thus providing reliable data about age effects. Cross-sectional studies may be confounded by the cohort effect and are not as valid for measuring age effects.

55. **B**—(Chapter 11) Their goal seems more related to successful completion of the course with a passing grade than learning the material. Grades represent extrinsic rewards, while learning for pleasure and internal satisfaction represent intrinsic rewards.

56. **B**—(Chapter 8) Repeated presentations of the conditioned stimulus without the unconditioned stimulus brings about extinction in classical conditioning. The conditioned response will disappear.

57. **B**—(Chapter 5) The median is a measure of central tendency achieved by ordering the numbers consecutively and determining the middle number. Here there are nine numbers, so the 5th number, 8, is the median of the scores.

58. **C**—(Chapter 9) Because the AP exam in Psychology is supposed to measure what you have learned in a course already taken, it is an achievement test.

18. Most New Yorkers in their thirties remember where they were and what they were doing when they heard that the World Trade Center was destroyed. Which of the following best identifies this type of memory?

   (A) implicit memory
   (B) engrams
   (C) flashbulb memory
   (D) explicit memory
   (E) déjà vu

19. Although a man watched in horror as his wife and children were killed by a speeding truck as they crossed the street, he has no memory of the event and gets upset when people tell him he must remember. The man is most likely suffering from

   (A) panic disorder
   (B) post-traumatic stress disorder
   (C) dissociative amnesia
   (D) bipolar disorder
   (E) deindividuation

20. According to the Law of Effect, behaviors followed by negative consequences

   (A) occur more frequently
   (B) occur less frequently
   (C) will never be performed again
   (D) will be performed more forcefully
   (E) are unpredictable

21. The pastry chef ordinarily makes 15 apple turnovers in 15 minutes, but when culinary arts students are watching him, he makes 20 apple turnovers in 15 minutes. This exemplifies

   (A) foot-in-the-door phenomenon
   (B) social loafing
   (C) social facilitation
   (D) the bystander effect
   (E) Type B behavior

22. The part of the neuron that directs synthesis of neurotransmitters and proteins is the

   (A) cell body
   (B) dendrite
   (C) axon
   (D) axon terminal
   (E) myelin sheath

23. According to Erikson, those who look back at the end of their lives with regrets and the feeling that their lives have lacked fulfillment evidence unsuccessful resolution of the challenge of

   (A) intimacy versus isolation
   (B) identity versus role confusion
   (C) integrity versus despair
   (D) generativity versus stagnation
   (E) industry versus inferiority

24. Which of the following is the most reliable indicator of emotions across all cultures?

   (A) hand gestures
   (B) facial expressions
   (C) voice intonation
   (D) body posture
   (E) smoothness of movements

25. The more difference shown by the behavior of identical twins raised apart, the more the differences in their behavior can be attributed to their

   (A) heritability
   (B) genetic traits
   (C) mutations
   (D) coincidence
   (E) environments

26. All public institutions subscribe to all of the following ethical guidelines EXCEPT

   (A) avoiding unnecessary deception to humans
   (B) avoiding unnecessary pain to humans and other animals
   (C) avoiding use of animals when computers are available
   (D) protecting confidentiality
   (E) having Institutional Review Boards approve all research conducted within their institutions

27. Mason is a fifth grader who tries to listen to the teacher but has difficulty focusing. He looks around the classroom while the teacher is talking and then does not know what to do when others are starting their assignments. These symptoms are characteristic of which of the following?

   (A) panic disorder
   (B) post-traumatic stress disorder
   (C) attention-deficit/hyperactivity disorder
   (D) bipolar disorder
   (E) antisocial personality disorder

GO ON TO THE NEXT PAGE

28. Joan strongly believes in capital punishment. After discussing capital punishment with only other people who believe in capital punishment in a chat room, Joan is most likely to

(A) believe more strongly in capital punishment
(B) believe less strongly in capital punishment
(C) not have changed her views at all
(D) want more information about capital punishment before deciding how strongly she supports capital punishment
(E) not want to discuss capital punishment any more

29. Answering multiple-choice questions is often easier than answering fill-in or completion questions, because multiple-choice questions

(A) provide more retrieval cues
(B) enhance retention of information
(C) check memorization rather than critical thinking
(D) are definitional rather than conceptual
(E) are easier to encode than completion questions

30. A neutral stimulus that signals an unconditioned stimulus begins to produce a response that anticipates and prepares for the unconditioned stimulus during

(A) acquisition trials
(B) generalization
(C) extinction trials
(D) spontaneous recovery
(E) operant conditioning

31. According to Jean Piaget, egocentrism, animism, and trial-and-error learning are characteristic of the stage of development known as

(A) preoperational
(B) sensorimotor
(C) concrete operational
(D) adolescence
(E) formal operational

32. Blinking, sneezing, flinching, and coughing are examples of the type of behavior called

(A) instinct
(B) reflex
(C) habit
(D) thought
(E) arc

33. Stephen is going through his second divorce. He thinks that no woman will ever love him again. His therapist points out to Stephen that his thinking is irrational and faulty. Which of the following therapies is the therapist employing?

(A) psychoanalysis
(B) systematic desensitization
(C) flooding
(D) rational emotive
(E) client-centered

34. Delia is deciding between a trip to Disney or Universal and is having difficulty choosing which amusement park to attend. With which of the following conflicts is she faced?

(A) frustration–aggression
(B) intrinsic–extrinsic
(C) approach–avoidance
(D) approach–approach
(E) avoidance–avoidance

35. EEGs that consist primarily of alpha and beta waves are characteristic of

(A) consciousness
(B) stage 1 sleep
(C) stage 2 sleep
(D) stage 3 sleep
(E) stage 4 sleep

36. A psychologist focusing on whether development occurs in stages is most interested in which of the following controversies?

(A) nature versus nurture
(B) continuity versus discontinuity
(C) stability versus change
(D) subjectivity versus objectivity
(E) individualism versus collectivism

37. Collective unconscious, archetypes, and individuation are personality concepts most closely associated with

(A) Sigmund Freud
(B) Carl Jung
(C) B. F. Skinner
(D) Karen Horney
(E) Albert Bandura

38. Which of the following is a hallucination?

    (A) thinking you are the president of the United States
    (B) being sure that your boss is out to get you
    (C) thinking this is 2013
    (D) feeling extraordinarily happy and agitated one moment, then extraordinarily depressed the next
    (E) hearing voices that are not actually there

39. Stella remembered the order of the planets from the Sun by recalling the sentence "My very educated mother just served us noodles." For Stella, this sentence is a

    (A) chunking strategy
    (B) mnemonic device
    (C) peg system
    (D) acoustic encoding sequence
    (E) proactive interference inhibitor

40. Which of the following is caused by a teratogen?

    (A) Tay-Sachs disease
    (B) Klinefelter's syndrome
    (C) Turner syndrome
    (D) Down syndrome
    (E) fetal alcohol syndrome

41. In classical conditioning the learner learns to associate the unconditioned stimulus with

    (A) an unconditioned response
    (B) a conditioned stimulus
    (C) a conditioned response
    (D) a negative reinforcer
    (E) a punishment

42. According to Selye's General Adaptation Syndrome (GAS) theory, of the following stages, we are most susceptible to disease during

    (A) resolution
    (B) resistance
    (C) alarm
    (D) exhaustion
    (E) extinction

43. Jeanette locked the front door and then checked it by turning the knob. She checked it a second time. After walking halfway down the path to the street, Jeanette went back to the door and checked to make sure that it was locked. Her behavior appears to be

    (A) psychotic
    (B) schizophrenic
    (C) obsessive
    (D) compulsive
    (E) manic

44. Carlos could consistently differentiate the note middle C on the violin from middle C on the piano because of the difference in

    (A) frequency
    (B) primary wavelength
    (C) amplitude
    (D) timbre
    (E) volume

45. Hunger, thirst, and sex are most closely associated with stimulation of the

    (A) pons
    (B) cerebellum
    (C) hypothalamus
    (D) temporal lobes
    (E) basal ganglia

46. For which of the following disorders might a psychiatrist prescribe a selective serotonin reuptake inhibitor such as Prozac or Paxil?

    (A) manic
    (B) depressive
    (C) dissociative identity
    (D) conversion
    (E) schizophrenic

GO ON TO THE NEXT PAGE

47. Jared thinks that going to psychology lecture classes is a waste of time and that you can do just as well in the course if you just read the review book, watch "Discovering Psychology," and take the tests. He decides to test his hypothesis with an experiment. The independent variable in his experiment is

    (A) going to lecture classes
    (B) going to lecture classes, reading the review book, and watching "Discovering Psychology"
    (C) not going to lecture classes, reading the review book, and watching "Discovering Psychology"
    (D) just taking tests
    (E) doing as well on tests without going to class as with going to class

48. In class, John's teacher tells him that she will give him the coin and bill for each picture he can correctly identify on the face of the penny, nickel, dime, quarter, half-dollar, dollar bill, and five-dollar bill. John cannot identify any of them, although he has been handling money for 17 years. His inability to remember the pictures most likely results from

    (A) confabulation
    (B) failure to reconstruct
    (C) failure to encode
    (D) deep processing
    (E) repression

49. Stranded in a deserted area after a boating accident, Harry was able to survive by eating leaves and insects and drinking water he boiled in a fire he made. According to Gardner's Theory of Multiple Intelligences, Harry displayed a high level of which of the following intelligences?

    (A) naturalistic
    (B) interpersonal
    (C) verbal-linguistic
    (D) mathematical
    (E) *g*

50. Menarche occurs at about age

    (A) 12 in males only
    (B) 12 in females only
    (C) 12 in both sexes
    (D) 12 in females and 14 in males
    (E) 50 in females only

51. Amy's therapist shakes her head affirmatively and says, "Yes, uh huh," as Amy talks about her problems. Which of the following treatments did she experience?

    (A) psychoanalysis
    (B) behavior therapy
    (C) humanistic therapy
    (D) cognitive therapy
    (E) existential therapy

52. Lucille suffered a stroke last week and cannot recognize her children or grandchildren by looking at them. Of the following structures, her brain lesion is most likely in the

    (A) cerebellum
    (B) hypothalamus
    (C) amygdala
    (D) left cerebral cortex
    (E) right cerebral cortex

53. According to the Gestalt organizing principles of perception, when you look at "i n car n a t e," you tend to notice the word *car* rather than *in*, *nate*, *at*, or *ate*, because of

    (A) continuity
    (B) the phi phenomenon
    (C) similarity
    (D) figure–ground
    (E) proximity

54. Which of the following is a secondary reinforcer?

    (A) food
    (B) water
    (C) money
    (D) sex
    (E) token economy

55. An action potential involves the movement of

    (A) glucose into the axon
    (B) fats out of the axon terminal
    (C) molecules in the synaptic gap
    (D) sodium ions into the axon
    (E) fluoride ions out of the axon

of the brain, which is specialized for visual/spatial reasoning.

86. **C**—(Chapter 8) The cognitive revision of Pavlovian classical conditioning is called the contingency model. Rescorla theorized that the predictability of the UCS following the presentation of the CS determines classical conditioning in contrast to Pavlov's contiguity model based on timing between the appearances.

87. **A**—(Chapter 11) Nomothetic theory analyzes personality characteristics according to universal norms of the group, in contrast to idiographic theory, which looks at the individual.

88. **A**—(Chapter 11) Relative deprivation theory is based on a cognitive model of motivation. How Tamika perceives her situation is changed once she works with those who have even less than she does.

89. **E**—(Chapter 9) Tests for which a person's performance can be compared with a pilot group. The pilot group, a representative group of the population to be tested, helps to establish a baseline so that the future performance of groups can be meaningfully compared and defined.

90. **A**—(Chapter 6) Acetylcholine is a neurotransmitter that causes contraction of skeletal muscles. In addition to this somatic task, it also helps regulate heart muscles, is involved in memory, and transmits messages between the brain and spinal cord. Alzheimer's is associated with a lack of this neurotransmitter.

91. **A**—(Chapter 10) Turning their heads toward stimuli when touched on their cheeks. This is one of a group of reflexive actions that is innate and present at birth.

92. **A**—(Chapter 5) The correlation coefficient is a statistical measure of the degree of relatedness between two sets of data that range from a +1 positive correlation (both increase together) to a −1 in this case, which represents a complete negative correlation (as one increases, the other decreases).

93. **D**—(Chapter 7) Electrical stimulation. Substance P is blocked by the endorphins, which are released by the electrical stimulation, thus blocking the pain sensation, according to the gate-control theory of pain.

94. **A**—(Chapter 9) Anchoring effect. Individuals are influenced by a suggested reference point or range, particularly when uncertain what amount to give. They base their giving on the "acceptable" range provided and thus will give more when the starting value is $25 rather than the "high" amount being $25.

95. **C**—(Chapter 7) Pressure receptors. A push is a form of mechanical energy. Mechanical energy is changed to the electrochemical energy of a neural impulse by pressure receptors of the skin.

96. **E**—(Chapter 7) Itch. Somatosensation is the perception of skin sensations (touch), which include cold, warm, pain, and pressure.

97. **B**—(Chapter 11) Increase in salivation. When one is aroused by a stressful situation like standing up and giving a speech in front of others, dry mouth, or a decrease in salivation, is often present.

98. **A**—(Chapter 7) Too much curvature of the cornea and lens. In nearsightedness, light rays are focused in front of the retina, causing distant objects to appear blurry.

99. **A**—(Chapter 6) Dissociation. According to Hilgard, a person undergoing hypnosis for pain management may feel little pain because the brain channel that registers pain is separated from channels registering the voice of the hypnotist. But a "hidden observer" can still observe his or her own pain without consciously experiencing any suffering.

100. **A**—(Chapter 5) Meta-analysis. This approach would compare and contrast all the studies as a group and thus determine trends and provide a greater understanding of the entire body of research on the herb and its effects on memory.

Section II
Scoring Rubric for Essay 1

This is a 10-point essay: 5 points are awarded for explaining at least one argument for the nature side of each of these issues and 5 points for explaining at least one argument for the nurture side of each of these.

Point 1: Shyness (Nature)

- Kagan's longitudinal research on inhibited children
- strong correlation between inhibited parents/grandparents and shy children
- cultural differences as a product of genetics

Point 2: Shyness (Nurture)

- 25 percent of Kagan's children changed temperament by adolescence
- collectivist societies promote modesty and shyness, respect for authority
- gender role socialization rewards females for shyness
- abused children, others with low self-esteem, or socially rejected may learn shyness
- according to Zimbardo, 50 percent of Americans self-report shyness
- cognitive behavioral therapy is successful in helping to overcome shyness

Point 3: Language acquisition (Nature)

- Noam Chomsky's "language acquisition device" in which grammar switches are turned on
- all children, including deaf children, babble at around 4 months and develop language in a distinct pattern: cooing, babbling, babbling only phonemes of their language group, holophrases, telegraphic speech
- overgeneralization of grammar rules by age 3, not influenced by formal training
- critical period hypothesis

Point 4: Language acquisition (Nurture)

- Skinner's argument of language acquisition through shaping
- deaf speech hindered because of an inability to hear proper sounds
- all children babble some 100 phonemes at 6 months, but by 10 months they use the phonemes only found in their language group, which obviously have been reinforced
- Whorf's language relativity hypothesis that languages shape the way we think
- failure of isolated children (such as Genie) to develop language

Point 5: Phenylketonuria (PKU) (Nature)

- inherited error of metabolism
- recessive gene, must have two alleles to be expressed
- high levels of phenylalanine lead to severe retardation and other problems

Point 6: Phenylketonuria (Nurture)

- screening at birth can alert adults to a lack of enzyme and need to avoid phenylalanine
- diet eliminating sources of phenylalanine (such as proteins, nuts, aspartame, and legumes) prevents expression of phenylketonuria

Point 7: Violent behavior (Nature)

- Freud's aggression instinct which leads to violent behavior
- higher testosterone levels or low levels of serotonin may predispose violence
- Delgado's stimulation studies

- adoption studies indicating violent children more like biological parents than adoptive parents

Point 8: Violent behavior (Nurture)

- Bandura's social learning theory, bobo doll studies
- correlation between violence and video game behavior
- negative consequence of violent upbringing—most abusers were abused by their parents
- receiving or expecting rewards for aggression—gang behavior and deindividuation

Point 9: Schizophrenia (Nature)

- exposure during pregnancy to flu virus and other teratogens leads to enlarged ventricles in brain
- age of expression seems to be 17–25 for most subtypes
- dopamine hypothesis, response to antipsychotic drugs that decrease dopamine
- high probability that monozygotic twin of twin with schizophrenia will develop schizophrenia
- high incidence of schizophrenia in close relatives

Point 10: Schizophrenia (Nurture)

- diathesis-stress model requires an environmental releaser
- milder cases of schizophrenia in less stressed twins
- Vietnam veteran syndrome—right age of onset and stressor strong enough

Sample Full-Credit Essay

The nature/nurture controversy has been one of the more enduring themes of psychological research. Although it used to be an either/or question of heredity or environment, now most psychologists agree with an interactionist point of view.

Jerome Kagan did some interesting longitudinal research with infants. By 2 months of age, 15 to 20 percent of children in his sample were already expressing inhibited behavior in the form of startle reactions to new stimuli. In their teens, 75 percent of his original group of inhibited kids were still inhibited. American parents who seem to value more extraverted behaviors were unable to change their children's nature. Strong correlations have been found between inhibited children and parents and grandparents as well.

Many people seem to learn shyness from abusive parenting styles, negative experiences in school, and rejection in social situations as both children and adults. Some 50 percent of Americans self-report shyness. Philip Zimbardo has spent much of his life conducting research and therapy for shyness. Cognitive-behavioral therapy has been successful in helping formerly shy people to learn new social skills and in reinforcing more positive self-statements.

Language acquisition has also had its nature and nurture supporters. Prominent on the nature side is linguist Noam Chomsky, who argues for a language acquisition device in the brain. He cites evidence of a progressive sequence of language acquisition from cooing, babbling, holophrases, and telegraphic speech to even overgeneralization of grammar rules unaffected by learning. Chomsky has indicated a critical period during which a child must be exposed to language for this maturational process to occur. Although B. F. Skinner would agree with the steps in the language acquisition process, he disagrees with Chomsky and believes that language is acquired through shaping and reinforcement. Although all children babble some 100 phonemes at about 6 months of age, at 10 months most are only using the phonemes of their own language, some 40 in English that have been reinforced.

Phenylketonuria or PKU is an inherited problem of metabolism. In order to be expressed, two recessive alleles for this trait must be present. Today, screening for this metabolic disorder is done at birth, and the mental retardation and other problems associated with it in the past have been considerably altered. Following a restricted diet, at least until adolescence, can prevent the expression of phenylketonuria. The diet eliminates proteins, nuts, and dairy products and severely restricts starches like bread and potatoes.

There are many theories on both the nature and nurture side about violent behavior. Both Freud and Lorenz believed that aggression is innate and the frustration-aggression hypothesis claims that violent behavior is a natural product of built-up frustration. High testosterone levels and lower serotonin levels have also supported a biological basis for violent behavior. Some studies have indicated that children more closely mimic their violent biological parents than their adopted parents. On the nurture side, Bandura's social learning theory and bobo doll studies indicate that violent behavior can be learned through modeling and imitation. Recent studies indicate that children who play violent video games are more likely to display violent behavior than those who do not play such games. Gangs who commit violent crimes reward similar behavior by their members and punish those who do not conform to these norms. Finally, in a highly aroused state, many people fall into a mob violence situation, as soccer matches and social protest marches have shown, exemplifying deindividuation.

Some psychologists also think the causes of schizophrenia are biological, whereas others think its causes are environmental. Schizophrenia is a devastating mental disorder involving delusional thinking, sensory hallucinations, and other psychotic symptoms. High levels of dopamine that can be treated with antipsychotic drugs in many cases seem to support the biological origin of this disease. Enlarged ventricles of the brain can be seen in MRIs or at autopsy. The disorder is most likely to express itself during the 17- to 25-year age period. Some theorize that mothers were exposed to flu-like viruses during their second trimester and that these factors lie dormant in the brain until late adolescence. Those arguing on the nurture side cite the diathesis-stress model and the double-bind situation. According to the double-bind theory, bad parenting makes the child confused about how to perceive the world. Twin studies in which one twin exhibits severe symptoms of schizophrenia and the other milder symptoms or none at all may be a result of environmental factors and stress levels—either real or perceived—that the two experience.

Scoring Rubric for Essay 2

Five points are to be awarded for the sensory and brain issues addressed in **a**, 2 points for explaining the "fight-or-flight" theory in **b**, and 1 point for correctly identifying and explaining a current theory of emotion in **c**.

Point 1: Eye focusing the image—cornea→pupil→lens→retina

Point 2: Eye transducing energy—rods and cones are photoreceptors that convert light energy to energy of the electrochemical impulse

Point 3: Transmission of information to the brain—from the retina→optic nerve→thalamus or brain

Points 4 and 5: Mention of at least two brain parts involved in visual processing of the bear: optic chiasma where information from one-half of each eye crosses to opposite hemisphere; thalamus as sensory relay and for color processing; occipital lobes or feature detectors in visual cortex; association areas of the cortex integrate sensory information to enable perception of bear

Point 6: Explanation of the "fight-or-flight" response—sympathetic nervous system increases heart rate, pulse, and blood pressure and slows digestion making energy available to muscles

Point 7: Pituitary signals adrenal glands to secrete adrenaline, which gives the extra surge of energy to run faster than ever

Point 8: Description of either Schachter's two-factor theory or Lazarus's cognitive appraisal theory or Ekman's facial feedback system or LeDoux and role of amygdala

Sample Essay

Seeing the brown bear in his backyard obviously caused an alarming sensory experience for John, which was quickly translated into quick action thanks to his sympathetic nervous system and the expression of fearful emotion. Light rays bounced off the bear's brown coat and entered John's eyes through the cornea, which begins the process of focusing. Next, the light passes through the pupil controlled by the iris. John's eyes open very wide! Next, the light is focused by the curved lens, which changes shape in relation to the distance of the bear and inverts the bear's image to focus on the retina on the back part of the eye where receptors (rods and cones) are stimulated. The rods and cones transduce the light energy into the electrochemical energy of a neural impulse. The brown color stimulates the cones especially concentrated in the fovea, which is where John's best acuity is. If enough cells fire, the bipolar cells are activated and finally the ganglion cells are activated. The axons of the ganglion cells in each eye form the optic nerves, which send the image to the thalamus in the brain (the sensory relay), which then sends it on to the occipital lobes where feature detectors will help John to perceive the dangerous image of the bear.

The "fight-or-flight" reaction is the physiological arousal of the body or sympathetic nervous system in response to a stressor (the bear) that enables John to get away fast. When John perceived the bear, messages were sent to his organs, glands, and muscles. John's heart rate and blood pressure immediately accelerated, and his breathing deepened. The pituitary gland also secreted hormones that commanded the adrenal glands to secrete adrenaline (epinephrine), which helped give him the extra energy to run faster than he had ever done.

There are several contemporary theories that are helpful in explaining why John felt fear and not anger or sadness. Schachter's two-factor model explains that first John felt the physiological arousal as explained earlier. He could identify the reason for this arousal (the bear) and knowing that bears can be very dangerous, he felt the emotion of fear. Lazarus's model says that a thought must come before any emotion or physiological arousal. John recognized that the bear could kill him, and then he could actually experience the fear. Ekman would explain the fear as the experience of changes in his facial muscles. When reacting to the bear, John's eyes widened, his teeth clenched, and these muscle cues alerted his brain to interpret this as fear. Anger or sadness would involve different muscles.

Day 3

When answering constructed response questions, follow this simple recipe:

- Define the term (even if the exam tells you definitions won't gain points) because it provides a simple start to your essay.

- Give an example of the term within a situation.

- Answer the question within the parameters set by the question itself.

5 Minutes to a 5

❮ 331

Day 4

CHAPTER 5. HISTORY AND APPROACHES

To understand the *Barnum Effect*, use a daily horoscope and switch the predictions for each of the astrological signs. Share the new "predictions" with classmates, friends, or family and observe the participants' likelihood to believe the interpretation.

Day 5

Spend a week observing and noting any coverage of psychology in the media (such as radio, TV, newspaper, movies, social media, etc.). Relate the news story to any terms you know in psychology.

Day 6

Research what happened in psychology on your birthday.

Day 7

Distinguish between Ancient Hebrews, Augustine, Locke, Socrates, Plato, Aristotle, and Descartes in terms of the relationship between mind and body.

Day 19

What is meant by the term *plasticity* when referring to the brain?

Describe the parts of a neuron.

Day 21

Explain how a neural impulse is generated.

Day 22

What is meant by the all-or-none response?

Day 23

Create a chart of the following neurotransmitters. Be sure to include the function, as well as what malfunctions may be associated with an under- or oversupply of each: acetylcholine, dopamine, GABA, glutamate, norepinephrine, serotonin.

Conduct a quick experiment to demonstrate sensory adaptation.

Day 36

Describe the nature of the wavelength and amplitude of light.

Explain how light energy is transduced to neural messages.

How do we see color?

Day 39

How is transduction accomplished in the inner ear?